From Divorce Mess
to Happiness

From Divorce Mess to Happiness

No-Nonsense Wisdom & Encouragement from Everyday People

Jen Fort

From the Wisdom & Warnings® book series

Other books in the Wisdom & Warnings series

The Badass Woman

Tips from the Quad

Let Then Fly

Because You Care

Happily Ever After

Our library of wisdom keeps growing!
Check out the full list anytime at wisdomandwarnings.com or
simply scan the QR code.

Disclaimer
The author of *From Divorce Mess to Happiness* is not a licensed therapist.
Because of this, this book is presented solely for educational and
entertainment purposes and is not intended to be a substitute for the advice
of a physician, professional coach, therapist, and other qualified
professionals.

This book was created with the assistance of various resources,
including AI as a brainstorming tool to help organize ideas and
enhance clarity. However, all insights, concepts, and creative content
are entirely the author's.

Dedication

This book is dedicated to my two adult children, Kendall and Steven, their father, Kevin, and my husband, Clive.

Kendall, thank you for always bringing sweetness and snuggles into our days. Steven, your humor and curiosity constantly kept me on my toes. Both of you were my anchors, reminding me to focus on creating a positive, joyful life, even when times were tough. Watching you both grow into such smart, compassionate, and lighthearted adults is a dream fulfilled. My heart overflows with love and pride for each of you.

Kevin, it might seem unusual to thank a former spouse, but I can't overlook your role in this journey. Despite the early challenges and uncomfortable moments, we've achieved something rare—we've remained friends while raising two incredible, well-adjusted humans. Thank you.

To my husband, Clive, thank you for encouraging me to pursue my passion for sharing life's wisdom and lessons. Your gentle nudges turned my idea into action and ultimately into this book. It simply wouldn't exist without you.
I love you.

What People Are Saying

"As a collaboratively trained divorce attorney and mediator dedicated to fostering positive outcomes, I am delighted to endorse "From Divorce Mess to Happiness." This remarkable book is an invaluable resource for anyone navigating the turbulent waters of divorce, offering daily encouragement and practical, real-life advice to help individuals find their way from heartbreak to hope. Divorce is a difficult emotional time for the individuals and the family. I have found in my practice that while going through a divorce, my clients are so emotionally charged it is hard for them to make decisions and move forward. Jen Fort captures the daily trials and tribulations of someone going through separation and divorce. Her insight helps one stay focused and motivated with manageable daily reflections.

"From Divorce Mess to Happiness" is infused with a sense of positivity and hope which is invaluable during this time in someone's life. It acknowledges the pain and complexity of divorce but always steers you towards the possibility of a happier, more fulfilling life. "From Divorce Mess to Happiness" is a must-read for anyone going through a divorce by offering the perfect blend of daily encouragement and practical advice, making it an ideal complement to the professional support of divorce lawyers, counselors, mediators, and financial advisors. I will give this book to all my clients as a must read."

—*Debra Forman, Divorce Attorney*

"If only I'd had this book as I tucked tail and ran out of my marriage after too many heart-wrenching failed attempts to build a bridge of understanding with my former spouse. The simple clarity and wisdom offered in this easy read book would have meant a world of difference to my experience. Who knows, it might even have preserved a friendship and left us both feeling heard."

—*Diane C.*

"I've been divorced twice, and this book would have been really helpful back then. This is a great resource not only for people who are divorcing, but the practical advice can be used for almost any situation where two people don't see eye to eye."

—*Wendy P.*

"I needed this book twenty years ago!"

—*Kathy K.*

Share Your Wisdom!

Wisdom & Warnings consists of nearly 8,000 carefully curated nuggets of wisdom across dozens of topics for life's milestones, ranging from relationships to parents/children to education and career, plus fun topics for living your best life.

Engage with the Wisdom & Warnings community for ongoing encouragement through life's milestones.

www.wisdomandwarnings.com
Facebook: https://www.facebook.com/wisdomandwarnings/
Instagram: @wisdomandwarnings
Email: hello@wisdomandwarnings.com

Table of Contents

How to Use This Book

Welcome!

If you are reading this book, you are either considering the end of your marriage or in the messy middle of the divorce process. Because divorce is incredibly challenging and unique to each person, it's easy to feel overwhelmed. I can say this because it was my personal experience and that of many people I've met along the way.

You might want to jump to the end and be finished with the season of divorce; however, the messy middle is where the mayhem or the magic happens, and no one can avoid it. You must travel through the season to get to the other side.

The contents of this book have been curated from my own life experience as well as from conversations with and observations of friends and strangers who shared their victories and struggles. Everyone I know who has experienced divorce, either firsthand or as an innocent ... or not-so-innocent ... bystander, has stories to tell about the lessons learned—actions taken in the heat of the moment that ended horribly or the kind gestures that made a world of difference toward a cooperative outcome.

For a moment, think if you have ever met someone who is friendly with their former partner and wondered, How do they do it? Or if you have observed former spouses sitting together, both supporting their child at a sporting or school event, you left being in awe of their friendship (or perceived friendship) and how the child beams to see both parents in the audience. I'm here to tell you, it can be done. One step at a time. One decision at a time. One pause before reacting. There are people, myself included, who have come through divorce with their sanity, pride, and well-being in one piece, and you can too. But it does take intention.

Day by day, this book will help you move closer to a peaceful dissolution of your marriage and provide encouragement for you to start your new life, having made peace with the past and hope for the future.

While From Divorce Mess to Happiness is organized in chapters based on the important phases of divorce, feel free to jump around. The goal of this book, and the entire Wisdom & Warnings project, is to share life lessons in a way that you can pick and choose which ones resonate with you and your situation. You may be surprised when you turn to a random page and the message is exactly what is needed.

This book is not a replacement for professional therapy. While the insights and wisdom shared here come from a place of love and understanding, they are meant to complement—not substitute—professional guidance. Divorce can trigger a wide range of emotions, from sadness and anger to relief and hope. In some cases, it can also bring deep-seated trauma and intense emotional pain to the surface. If you are experiencing severe, emotional distress, trauma, or any extreme situation, I strongly urge you to seek professional support. Therapists, counselors, and other mental health professionals can help you navigate these complexities with the care and expertise you deserve.

Think of this book as a companion on your journey—a friend offering a shoulder to lean on and a gentle nudge toward positivity. Professional support, on the other hand, is all about having a skilled guide who can help you navigate the most treacherous parts of your path, ensuring you find your way safely. Remember, asking for help is a sign of strength, not weakness. It takes courage to recognize when you need support, and even more so to seek it out. Your well-being is super important to me, and there is no shame in reaching out to those who can help you through this challenging time.

Take care of yourself, dear reader. You are worthy of all the support and kindness this world has to offer.

With love and encouragement,
Jen

Chapter 1
The Big Decision: Do I Stay or Do I Go?

Day 1

*There is a difference between giving up and
knowing when you have had enough.*

While some people may view divorce as giving up, others recognize that there comes a point when continuing to persevere in a troubled relationship can be more detrimental than beneficial. Knowing when you've had enough requires a profound understanding of your needs, boundaries, and well-being. It entails acknowledging that, despite your best efforts and intentions, some relationships may simply not be salvageable. Deciding to divorce is an act of self-preservation and courage, showing a willingness to prioritize your mental, emotional, and, sometimes, physical health. It's about recognizing your worth and dignity and refusing to settle for a situation that compromises your happiness and fulfillment. Knowing when you've had enough is an empowering act of self-love and self-respect.

Day 2

*Do some real soul-searching to understand
why the marriage is ending.*

Before deciding to divorce, it's important to do some genuine soul-searching to comprehend the reasons behind the unraveling of the marriage. This self-reflection isn't about assigning blame or pointing fingers; it's about digging deep into your own heart and mind to unearth the underlying issues. Take the time to reflect on your feelings, desires, and aspirations. While you're at it, also explore the dynamics of the relationship, acknowledging both the highs and lows. This information will be critical to all future relationships.

Day 3

*If you're not 100% sure divorce is the answer, suggest a
trial separation to give each other time and space.*

If you are wavering in your decision to divorce, consider proposing a trial separation. This temporary time apart allows both of you to gain clarity, perspective, and emotional space. It offers a chance to reflect on the dynamics of the relationship and assess whether reconciliation is possible or if divorce is indeed the best course of action. While the outcome may vary, a trial separation can serve as a valuable catalyst for self-discovery and mutual understanding, ultimately leading to a resolution that aligns with the needs and desires of you both.

Day 4

The moment you stay silent about what truly matters is the moment you begin to lose yourself.

When you hold back from voicing your needs, desires, and concerns, you're inadvertently putting your happiness and fulfillment at stake. Repeated dismissals or neglect may have left you feeling undervalued in the relationship. With each instance of silence, the bond you share weakens, slowly chipping away at the very foundation it was built upon. By summoning the courage to break that silence and address reality, you take the first step toward regaining control over your life. Remember, your voice holds the key to reshaping, understanding, and nurturing mutual respect.

Day 5

Strength is not measured by holding on but by letting go.

Divorce will confront you with the agonizing choice between holding on and letting go. While the instinct to cling to familiarity and security can be powerful, true strength lies in the ability to release what no longer serves you. Letting go doesn't imply weakness; rather, it signifies courage and resilience. It requires acknowledging the pain and uncertainty of parting ways, but also recognizing the potential for growth and renewal that lies beyond.

Day 6

Sometimes doors close because it's time to move on

Even if you did not initiate the divorce, the closing of doors can feel like divine intervention prompting a significant move. It's as though the Universe recognized you would not embrace change unless circumstances forced you to. These closed doors signify an opportunity for growth, a signal that it's time to bid farewell to the past and step into a new chapter of your life. While it may initially feel daunting, this nudging from the Universe serves as a gentle reminder, or a kick in the pants, that sitting still is not an option.

Day 7

If you want a peaceful divorce, you must be at peace with ending the marriage.

Holding onto bitterness, resentment, or anger only prolongs the pain and conflict, making the divorce process more difficult for everyone involved. By making peace, you free yourself from the emotional baggage that may otherwise cloud your judgment and block constructive communication with your soon-to-be ex-spouse. It's not about forgetting the past or pretending everything was perfect; it's about embracing imperfections and choosing to let go with grace and dignity.

Day 8

Your life is a story. Your past is one chapter. Your future has yet to be written.

Imagine your life as a book brimming with countless chapters, each narrating its tale of highs and lows. Your marriage makes up just one of these chapters, composed of many pages filled with both joy and sorrow. Divorce marks another chapter in your journey, and soon it will be in the past. Recognizing that the stories of yesterday have no control over your present or future sets you free. Embracing release cultivates a sense of tranquility amidst the tumult of separation and divorce. Saying goodbye to a marriage demands courage, yet it offers the promise of fresh opportunities to write the story of your life on your own terms. Listen to your heart, but don't forget to bring your mind along.

Day 9

Follow your heart but take your brain with you.

Following your heart feels good. It allows you to honor your deepest desires and values, guiding you toward decisions aligned with your authentic self. However, by tempering your emotional impulses with logical reasoning, you will navigate the complexities of divorce with clarity and foresight. It's the delicate balance between intuition and intellect that will empower you to make sound decisions amidst the chaos, leading you toward resolutions that serve your highest good.

Day 10

*Divorce isn't such a tragedy...
staying in an unhappy marriage.*

When you stay in an unhappy marriage, you sacrifice your well-being and compromise your ability to live a fulfilling life. The emotional toll from enduring constant conflict, dissatisfaction, and lack of fulfillment can lead to feelings of resentment, depression, and low self-worth. Staying in an unhappy marriage can perpetuate a cycle of dysfunction and unhappiness, affecting not only you but also any children or family members caught in the crossfire. Staying in an unhappy marriage prevents you from pursuing authentic happiness, personal growth, and meaningful connections with others.

Day 11

*Failure is simply the Universe giving you the
opportunity to start over, but with greater wisdom.*

There are always parts of a marriage that were successful and times when you enjoyed the partnership. You are now offered the chance to reassess, recalibrate, and begin again, armed with the wisdom learned from past experiences. As you navigate the complexities of divorce, each stumble and setback becomes an opportunity to chart a wiser course forward. Learn from mistakes, refine your approach, and embrace the lessons that adversity teaches you.

Day 12

*It might sound silly, but make sure your marriage
is truly over before you initiate divorce.*

Remember, words cannot be unsaid, and bells cannot be unrung. It's essential to take as much time as necessary to reflect on the state of your marriage to assess whether reconciliation is still a viable option and to explore all avenues of resolution before committing to divorce. This involves honest introspection, open communication with your partner, and perhaps seeking guidance from a trusted counselor or mediator. I encourage you to approach the process with clarity and conviction, minimizing regrets and maximizing the potential for a smoother transition and eventual closure for both of you.

Day 13

Never believe someone else knows what's best for you.

While well-meaning friends, family members, and even professionals will offer advice and guidance, ultimately, you are the expert on your life and circumstances. Trusting your instincts and intuition is crucial as you navigate the complexities of separation and make decisions that align with your values, priorities, and goals. What works for one person may not be the right choice for you, and vice versa. Stay true to yourself and honor your inner wisdom.

Day 14

Don't avoid hard decisions as they are usually the most impactful ... take them seriously.

It can be tempting to shy away from hard decisions. However, it's crucial to confront these challenges head-on, as they often carry the most weight in shaping your future. Whether it's determining custody arrangements, dividing assets, or establishing financial agreements, these choices will have a profound impact on your life post-divorce. By facing them directly and taking them seriously, you empower yourself to make informed decisions that align with your priorities.

Day 15

If you are going to overcome any challenge, you must first confront it.

There will come a time when you must acknowledge and accept the reality of your unraveled marriage. This first acknowledgment resembles stepping into the unknown, where uncertainty looms and emotions run high. However, confronting the truth head-on is like illuminating a path through the darkness—a crucial step toward resolution and eventual healing. Denying the existence of the challenges posed by divorce only serves to prolong the journey toward resolution. Instead, by embracing the truth of the situation, you will lay the groundwork for personal growth and empowerment.

Day 16

Decide how you want to divorce before you file.

Divorce is a significant life event, and how you and your partner approach it can have lasting effects. Take the time to reflect on your options and decide the method of divorce that best aligns with your needs and goals. Whether it's through mediation, collaborative divorce, or traditional litigation, each approach carries its own set of advantages and considerations. By choosing a method that prioritizes cooperation, communication, and mutual respect, you can mitigate conflict and minimize the emotional and financial toll of divorce.

Day 17

Sometimes, the smallest step in the right direction ends up being the biggest step of your life.

Despite the daunting nature of the path ahead, it's essential to muster the courage to move forward, even if it means tiptoeing cautiously. Each tiny step toward positive change, whether it's seeking therapy, initiating a tough conversation, or simply allowing yourself to feel and process your emotions, has the potential to lead to significant transformation. While the journey may feel overwhelming at times, it's important to remember that taking one small step at a time can often lead to progress. What small step will you take today?

Day 18

*If you choose to give up, make sure it's only
because you're starting over.*

If you are contemplating ending your marriage, be sure to have an equal commitment to embracing a journey of self-renewal. It's about recognizing that the ending of one chapter paves the way for a fresh start. By choosing to walk away, you're not just closing a chapter; you're opening a whole new book of possibilities. So, if you find yourself at the crossroads of a failing relationship, remember that it's okay to let go. But do it with the intention of rebuilding a life that aligns with your true self.

Day 19

*Just because someone desires you does
not mean they value you.*

The end of a marriage often forces individuals to reassess their self-worth and relationships. It's a time when one realizes that mere desire or attraction does not equate to genuine respect, appreciation, or commitment. While it's natural to seek validation and affection, settling for someone who merely desires you without valuing your worth can lead to further heartache and disappointment. By embracing this realization, you can cultivate healthier, more fulfilling connections in the future, grounded in genuine appreciation and understanding.

Day 20

There is great power in letting go, and
great freedom in moving on.

In the storm that is divorce, it can be challenging to see beyond the pain and envision a brighter future. By embracing the power of letting go, you will release yourself from bitterness and resentment that connects you to your past. Moving on from a divorce doesn't mean forgetting the past or denying one's emotions; rather, it involves acknowledging the pain, learning from it, and consciously choosing to create a new chapter filled with possibility and freedom.

Day 21

You are worthy of love and respect. You are
beautiful, gifted, and intelligent.

It's natural to question your worthiness of love and respect, especially in the wake of a failed relationship. However, it's crucial to remember that everyone deserves love and respect, regardless of their relationship status. Knowing you are worthy of love and respect serves as a powerful affirmation of your inherent value as a human being. It should remind you that your worth is not defined by your marital status or the opinions of others, but rather by your intrinsic qualities and unique contributions to the world. You are encouraged to set boundaries, prioritize your well-being, and surround yourself with people who are uplifting and supportive.

Day 22

Even in the darkest moments, happiness is possible if you look for the light.

Whether it's finding peace in cherished memories, leaning on the support of loved ones, or pursuing newfound passions, there are avenues to light even in the bleakest of situations. Turning on the light amidst darkness doesn't mean denying the pain or glossing over the difficulties of divorce. Instead, it's about actively seeking moments of brightness and cultivating resilience in the face of adversity.

Day 23

If you've given it your all, move forward with no regrets.

Divorce often carries a heavy burden of guilt and remorse with it, leaving questions about whether you could have done more to salvage the relationship. However, if you've given it your all, it's easier to move forward with a sense of closure and peace instead of regrets. It serves as a reminder that, despite the outcome, you should take solace in the fact that you poured your heart and soul into the marriage, leaving no stone unturned in your efforts to make it work. By acknowledging that you gave it your best, you can release the weight of self-blame and accept that some things are simply beyond your control. Shift your focus toward healing and moving forward with a clear conscience.

Day 24

Sometimes, all you must do is forget how you feel and remember what you deserve.

Amidst the chaos, it's crucial to maintain clarity and perspective, reminding yourself of your inherent value and deservingness of respect, love, and happiness. Despite the pain and turmoil experienced, resist the temptation to define yourself solely by emotions, and instead, focus on what you truly deserve in life. This means letting go of negative feelings and embracing a mindset that prioritizes self-respect, dignity, and empowerment. If you're struggling to discern what you deserve, consider the advice you would offer a cherished friend facing a similar situation. Sometimes, flipping the script and viewing your circumstances through the lens of compassionate guidance can offer valuable insight. By embracing this approach, you can cultivate a sense of self-worth and clarity that empowers you to navigate the challenges of divorce with resilience and grace.

Day 25

*Being single is better than being lied to,
cheated on, and disrespected.*

While being single may bring its own set of challenges, it can also offer a newfound sense of freedom, independence, and self-discovery. Choosing to prioritize one's well-being over remaining in a toxic or unhealthy relationship is an act of self-love and empowerment. It allows you to reclaim your autonomy and dignity, refusing to tolerate dishonesty, infidelity, or disrespect. By embracing the single life, you can focus on healing from past wounds and rediscovering your self-worth.

Day 26

*If someone is stupid enough to walk away,
be smart enough to let them go.*

Holding onto someone who chooses to leave ultimately prolongs the pain and prevents both individuals from moving forward. Choosing to release someone who walked away requires strength and self-awareness. It's a testament to valuing one's own worth and refusing to settle for less than genuine love and mutual respect. By acknowledging that someone who doesn't appreciate your worth isn't worth your time or energy, you empower yourself to seek healthier relationships in the future.

Day 27

It's better to have nobody than to have someone who is half there or doesn't want to be there at all.

Choosing solitude over a partnership where the other person is emotionally absent or unwilling to fully commit can lead to a healthier sense of self-worth and emotional well-being. It's better to prioritize your own happiness and emotional fulfillment rather than settle for a relationship that lacks depth or mutual respect. By valuing yourself enough to walk away from a relationship that doesn't meet your needs, you are paving the way for more meaningful connections in the future and cultivating a sense of inner strength and resilience that will serve you well on the journey ahead.

Day 28

Not everyone in your life is meant to stay.

Recognizing that not everyone who enters your life is meant to stay can be a challenging but liberating realization. It's essential to understand that clinging to relationships that no longer serve your well-being can hinder personal growth and prevent you from embracing new opportunities for happiness and fulfillment. While the end of a marriage may bring feelings of loss and uncertainty, it also presents an opportunity to reassess priorities, rediscover personal identity, and cultivate healthier connections with yourself and others.

Day 29

You can still love someone and be wrong for them.

Sometimes, despite your best intentions and efforts, you may find yourself in situations where the love you have for someone is simply not enough to overcome fundamental differences or incompatible dynamics. Accepting this reality can be challenging, but it's a crucial step toward prioritizing self-respect and honoring your needs and boundaries.

Day 30

It's better to be alone for the right reasons
than with someone for the wrong.

While the prospect of solitude may seem daunting, it pales in comparison to the toll that staying in an unsatisfying or unhealthy relationship can take on one's well-being. Embracing solitude allows individuals the opportunity to rediscover themselves, pursue their passions, and cultivate a sense of inner fulfillment. It's a chance to prioritize personal growth and create a life that aligns with your values and aspirations. While the journey may be challenging at times, the freedom and authenticity that comes with being true to yourself far outweighs the temporary discomfort of solitude.

Day 31

Sometimes, life gives you two options: losing yourself or losing the one you love. Don't lose yourself.

While the temptation to cling to the familiarity of a partnership may be strong, losing sight of your identity and needs can have detrimental consequences. It's crucial to remain grounded in your values, aspirations, and sense of worth. By choosing to prioritize self-care and authenticity, you can navigate divorce with resilience and integrity. Although the journey toward self-discovery and empowerment may be fraught with uncertainty and pain, keeping a steadfast commitment to personal growth ultimately leads to greater fulfillment and inner peace.

Day 32

The more knowledgeable you are going into a divorce, the more likely you will know what doesn't seem right.

By educating yourself about the legalities, procedures, and potential pitfalls of divorce, you gain the insight needed to recognize red flags, ask questions, and advocate for your rights. This knowledge equips you to find discrepancies and inconsistencies, enabling you to make informed decisions and assert your interests throughout the process. It also provides a framework for knowing when to pause, seek clarification, or add support.

Day 33

Sometimes, you must accept the truth and stop wasting time on the wrong person.

Continuing to invest time and energy in toxic or unhealthy relationships can hinder your ability to heal and move forward. By acknowledging the reality of the situation and letting go of attachments to the wrong person, you create space for new opportunities and healthier connections to enter your life. It's essential to prioritize your emotional health and surround yourself with individuals who support your growth and happiness. While it may be challenging to distance yourself from certain individuals, doing so allows you to cultivate a sense of empowerment and self-respect. Ultimately, accepting the truth about relationships after divorce enables you to focus on building a fulfilling and authentic life for yourself, free from unnecessary emotional baggage and negativity.

Chapter 2
Preparation Is Everything: Plan for the Worst, Work for the Best

Day 34

Sometimes, we must let go of what's killing us, even if it's killing us to let go.

In the aftermath of divorce, there are often aspects of the past that continue to weigh heavily on our hearts and minds. It can be incredibly challenging to release these burdens, especially when they have become intertwined with your sense of identity and well-being. However, holding onto pain and resentment only serves to prolong your suffering and prevent you from fully embracing the present moment. Sometimes, the most courageous act you can undertake is to let go of the people, memories, or emotions that are causing you harm, even if it feels agonizing to do so. By relinquishing your grip on what no longer serves you, you create space for healing, growth, and new beginnings.

Day 35

*Scrub and neutralize all social media of anything
negative regarding your relationship or spouse.
This goes for snarky memes too!*

It may be difficult, but it's extremely important to not share personal details, comment on divorce-related matters, or vent your frustrations on social media platforms. Instead, keep a discreet and dignified presence online, focusing on positive and uplifting content that reflects your resilience and strength. This may feel disingenuous, but remember, what you share online can have far-reaching negative consequences, so it's essential to approach social media with mindfulness and discretion during this sensitive time.

Day 36

*Don't ask for anything you are not ready for
and willing to accept for yourself.*

Before asking questions, it's crucial to assess your emotional preparedness and willingness to accept the answers, regardless of how they may affect you. Delving into sensitive topics prematurely can open wounds and hinder the healing process. Instead, focus on your journey toward healing and acceptance, allowing yourself the time and space to come to terms with the realities of divorce at your own pace.

Day 37

Now is not the time to detach and wing it.

The temptation to detach emotionally, stick your head in the sand, and simply "wing it" may be strong, but now is not the time for haphazard decision-making. Instead, it's crucial to dive into the details, educate yourself on the intricacies of the process, and make deliberate, well-informed choices. Each decision you make during this time can have long-lasting repercussions, so it's essential to proceed thoughtfully and methodically. Resist the urge to rush through the process or leave important matters to chance.

Day 38

Doing research does not guarantee you will get divorced; it just means you're becoming informed.

When faced with the prospect of divorce, knowledge is power. Transitioning into information-gathering mode allows you to arm yourself with essential insights about preparing for divorce, understanding the legal process, and navigating the often-turbulent emotions that accompany such a significant life change. Engaging in research and seeking resources does not signify a commitment to divorce; rather, it reflects an initiative-taking approach to understanding your options and rights.

Day 39

Don't be passive; take control of the process.

Rather than being a passive bystander, recognize that this is your divorce, and you hold the reins. Seizing ownership of the process empowers you to make decisions aligned with your needs, values, and aspirations. It means advocating for your interests, communicating your desires clearly, and actively taking part in negotiations and discussions. Embracing your role as the protagonist in your divorce narrative enables you to steer the course of proceedings toward a resolution that reflects your priorities and helps your healing and closure journey.

Day 40

Even if you've not handled the household finances before, now is the time to get up close and personal.

Understanding your financial situation empowers you to make informed decisions about asset division, spousal support, and future financial planning. Take the time to review bank statements, investment accounts, and any relevant legal documents to gain clarity on your financial standing. Don't be shy about consulting with a financial advisor or accountant to make sure you have a firm understanding of your financial rights and responsibilities.

Day 41

Open checking and savings accounts and one credit card in only your name.

As you step into this new chapter of your life, having your own bank account and funds for initial expenses is key. Plus, having your own accounts helps build your credit score. When you're the sole account holder, there's a comforting sense of security in knowing your ex can't dip into your funds or run up debts. By separating your finances, you're taking charge of your money, which is vital for your financial health and independence.

Day 42

You have the power to choose the process.

Rather than allowing circumstances to dictate the course of your divorce, empower yourself to make deliberate choices that align with your values, priorities, and desired outcomes. You can select the approach that best suits your needs, whether it be mediation, collaboration, or traditional litigation. By taking an active role in choosing the process, you take a stand and shape the trajectory of your divorce journey. Taking initiative allows you to focus on finding a peaceful solution, reducing conflicts, and prioritizing the well-being of yourself and your family.

Day 43

Make copies of all documents and keep them safe.

Take immediate action to safeguard financial documents by making copies and storing them in a secure location, preferably offsite. Gathering and duplicating essential documents, such as bank statements, tax returns, investment accounts, property deeds, and insurance policies, is crucial during divorce preparation. These documents serve as vital evidence of your financial standing and are essential for correct asset division and settlement negotiations. By keeping copies in a safe and separate location, you also protect yourself against potential loss, damage, or tampering.

Day 44

Safeguard your irreplaceable items.

It's important to safeguard irreplaceable items that hold emotional value. To ensure their protection, consider storing them in a secure location away from the marital home; at a trusted friend or family member's house or in a safety deposit box, for example. The goal is not to hide the items, as they will need to be accounted for during the division of assets, but you will have peace of mind knowing they are safe. Document these items thoroughly through photographs or written descriptions to prove their existence and value.

Day 45

A peaceful divorce isn't the same as a happy divorce.

A peaceful divorce simply implies a lack of conflict and animosity, facilitating a smoother transition and minimizing emotional turmoil. However, it does not guarantee feelings of joy or contentment. It's important to acknowledge that divorce is a challenging and often painful process, regardless of how amicable the proceedings may be. Despite the absence of conflict and knowing that happiness is on the horizon, you may still grapple with feelings of sadness, grief, and uncertainty as you navigate the end of a significant chapter in your life.

Day 46

DIY divorce can increase the likelihood of mistakes.

While straightforward divorces with minimal assets and no children may be suitable for a do-it-yourself approach, the likelihood of errors and oversights escalates as the complexity of the situation increases. Factors, such as shared assets, child custody, and spousal support agreements, require careful consideration and legal expertise to ensure fair outcomes. Without the guidance of a qualified legal representation, you may risk making mistakes that could have long-lasting consequences, including financial losses and prolonged legal battles.

Day 47

With mediation, you both are in the driver's seat.

The hands-on approach of mediation empowers couples to make informed decisions about important issues, such as asset division, child custody, and spousal support, without the intervention of a judge or lengthy court proceedings. By fostering open dialogue and minimizing the potential for miscommunication, mediation helps to ease tension and conflict, paving the way for more amicable resolutions. Respectful communication and keeping a level head are key to mediation.

Day 48

Mediation allows you to keep a level of trust and is helpful if there are children involved.

Mediation provides a structured environment for discussing parenting arrangements, addressing concerns, and developing strategies for effective co-parenting. By prioritizing the needs of your children and embracing open communication, mediation can help lay the groundwork for a successful co-parenting relationship, ensuring that your children thrive amidst the challenges of divorce.

Day 49

Look to mediation to end the marriage amicably.

With the guidance of a trained mediator, you and your spouse can engage in open dialogue, find common goals, and work toward a resolution that meets both of your needs while navigating the complexities of divorce with dignity and respect. Embracing a collaborative approach allows you to preserve relationships, minimize conflict, and lay the groundwork for a smoother transition into the next phase of your life. If both of you are committed and willing, engaging in mediation can minimize conflict, enabling you to move on more easily.

Day 50

Money surprises are never good.

Diligently recording your financial transactions allows you to gain insight into where your money is going and find areas for savings or budget adjustments. A financial journal can also serve as a valuable resource for your attorney, providing documentation of your financial history and supporting your case for fair asset division or child and/or spousal support. Whether it's through handwritten notes or a spreadsheet, keeping a financial journal ensures that you clearly understand your financial situation and enables you to make informed decisions about your future post-divorce.

Day 51

Divorce does not create income; it creates expense.

Let's be honest ... divorce will create new expenses that can strain your finances. Post-divorce, you may find that certain expenses, such as car insurance, cell phone plans, and even taxes, become more costly as you transition to single life. Additionally, legal fees and costs associated with dividing assets and setting up separate households can create even more financial tension. Carefully assessing your financial situation and planning accordingly is essential to mitigate the impact of these additional expenses.

Day 52

Prepare for the eventual rainy day by adding money to the bank accounts that are in your name only!

It's crucial to start a rainy-day fund as soon as possible. You can do this by adding money to a dedicated bank account just for you or stashing away cash in a secure spot. This fund acts as your safety net during the whirlwind of divorce, giving you a buffer for unexpected expenses or emergencies. Picture needing to cover the first month's rent for a new place or handle other initial costs tied to setting up your own household—your rainy-day fund is there to save the day. Without this fund, you might make choices based on tight finances that you'll regret later.

Day 53

Order an updated credit report now!

You can order a free credit report once a year from each of these three companies: Equifax, Experian, and TransUnion at www.annualcreditreport.com. Your credit report provides a comprehensive overview of your credit history and score, allowing you to assess your financial health and find any potential discrepancies or errors. Consider enrolling in a credit monitoring service to receive prompt alerts about any attempts to open new accounts or fraudulent activity in your name.

Day 54

Get your personal and marital finances organized as anything and everything will likely come into play.

Take the time to compile a comprehensive list of all assets and liabilities, including bank accounts, investments, real estate, vehicles, and debts. Don't overlook less obvious assets, such as work-related bonuses, perks, memberships, and reward points, which may hold significant value and be subject to division during divorce proceedings. These less obvious assets are a good place to look when negotiating asset division, so it's good to know everything you have.

Day 55

Attend financial planning seminars.

Financial planning seminars can offer invaluable insight and guidance on managing your finances effectively during and after divorce. Topics covered may include budgeting, asset management, debt reduction, and planning. In addition, you can network with others going through similar experiences, providing you with a support system and shared knowledge. Whether you're seeking strategies to protect your assets, plan for retirement, or establish a new financial framework post-divorce, these seminars offer a wealth of information to empower you to make informed decisions and secure your financial future.

Day 56

*Make sure you have and/or update your
Power of Attorney and Living Will.*

Now's the time to ensure that you have important legal documents in place to protect your interests and wishes. A Power of Attorney appoints someone to make decisions on your behalf if you become incapacitated. A Living Will outlines your healthcare preferences and treatment wishes in case you cannot express them due to illness or injury. This gives you peace of mind knowing that your affairs and healthcare decisions are in capable hands ... and not your former spouse's!

Day 57

Even the most peaceful divorce will be painful.

The decision to end a marriage marks a significant transition in life, often bringing about a range of emotions, including sadness, grief, and uncertainty. Despite efforts to maintain civility and cooperation throughout the divorce proceedings, the reality of separating lives and redefining relationships can be deeply challenging. It's important to acknowledge and validate the emotional upheaval that accompanies divorce, recognizing that healing and adjusting to change take time. Just like no two divorces are the same, neither is the healing process. You are on your own journey.

Day 58

You can expect an emotional rollercoaster.

It's entirely normal to experience an array of emotions during this challenging time. The dissolution of a marriage is a significant life transition, stirring up complex feelings as you grapple with the loss of the relationship, adjust to new realities, and confront the uncertainties of the future. Your emotional response to divorce is unique and is influenced by personal experiences, circumstances, and coping mechanisms. While the intensity and fluctuations of emotions may feel overwhelming at times, it's important to remember that all emotions are a natural part of the grieving and healing process.

Day 59

Learn all you can about the divorce process.

Understanding the legal procedures, your rights, and responsibilities involved can help you navigate negotiations more effectively and make informed decisions that prioritize your well-being and interests. Being well-informed allows you to engage in constructive communication with your former spouse, fostering a more cooperative and amicable atmosphere for resolving disputes. You will also have confidence that you have enough knowledge to be aware if someone is trying to take advantage of you or the situation.

Day 60

What will your new life cost? Don't get caught off guard!

Transitioning to a single-income household, dividing assets, and potentially paying alimony or child support can significantly affect one's financial stability. Carefully assessing your current and future financial needs is essential to avoid being caught off guard by unexpected expenses. Creating a detailed budget that accounts for living expenses, legal fees, and any added costs associated with starting a new life can help you better understand your financial situation and make informed decisions during the divorce process.

Day 61

Divorce is a marathon, not a sprint.

Just as marathon runners pace themselves to conserve energy and overcome obstacles along the way, individuals going through a divorce must adopt a similar mindset. It's essential to recognize that the journey will be filled with ups and downs, challenges, and triumphs, and it's crucial to maintain a focus on your long-term goals despite the immediate difficulties. By pacing yourself, seeking support from loved ones, and staying committed to the process, you can navigate through the complexities of divorce with greater endurance and ultimately emerge stronger and more resilient on the other side.

Day 62

Do not post anything that you would not want your ex, a judge, your mom, or your kids to see.

Posting content that may be inappropriate or incriminating can have significant repercussions on various aspects of the divorce process. It's essential to consider the potential impact of online activity on all parties involved, including your ex-spouse, legal authorities, family members, and children. By refraining from sharing content that your ex or a judge could misconstrue and use against you, you can avoid unnecessary conflicts and keep a level of professionalism and dignity throughout the divorce process.

Day 63

Reflect on the stability of your job and your former spouse's job, especially if you are relying on support.

Assessing the stability of employment helps predict potential changes in income and financial obligations, allowing for better planning and decision-making. If either party's job situation is uncertain, it may affect support arrangements, property division, and overall financial stability post-divorce. Reflecting on job stability can also inform negotiations about child support, spousal support, and other financial agreements, ensuring that arrangements are feasible and sustainable.

Day 64

The more you spend on your divorce, the less money you'll have to start your new life.

Legal fees, court costs, and other expenses associated with divorce can quickly add up, potentially draining valuable resources that could otherwise support your children and establish a new life post-divorce. By being mindful of your spending during the divorce proceedings, you can prioritize the well-being of your children and ensure that you have sufficient financial resources to meet their needs both now and in the future.

Day 65

Maintain a separate email account exclusively for communication regarding divorce.

Creating a separate email account for divorce research is a proactive step to protect your privacy and keep things confidential. By compartmentalizing your divorce-related communications and resources, you create a safe space for exploring sensitive topics and seeking support without fear of intrusion or judgment from anyone who might have access to the account.

Day 66

Consider getting a post office box and forwarding your mail to it so you don't lose important paperwork.

One practical step to safeguard important documents is to consider getting a PO Box and having all mail sent there. A PO Box provides a reliable mailing address that stays consistent, even if you move or change residences during the divorce proceedings. This stability can be valuable during a time of transition and upheaval. In addition, having a separate mailing address can help keep boundaries and reduce potential conflicts with your former spouse regarding mail delivery.

Day 67

Change passwords to critical accounts.

One effective measure to safeguard your personal data is to change passwords on critical accounts as soon as possible. These accounts may include email, banking, social media, and any other platforms that have confidential or sensitive information. By changing passwords, you can prevent unauthorized access to your accounts and ensure that your personal data remains secure. You can also consider enabling two-factor authentication for an added layer of security. This extra step helps to verify your identity when logging into accounts by requiring a code that they will send to your mobile device or email address, further reducing the risk of unauthorized access.

Sometimes, it might not be feasible to change the password. If you are concerned about your spouse removing assets, take a screenshot of account balances so you have proof of the assets when it comes time to divide them. Keeping the lines of communication wide open shows you're being upfront and respectful.

Day 68

Beginning a new relationship before your divorce is finalized can have negative consequences.

In certain states, the court might use your new relationship against you, creating negative consequences during the divorce proceedings. This aspect of the law varies by jurisdiction, so it's important to consult with your legal team or attorney to understand the specific regulations and guidelines in your state. Your legal counsel can provide valuable insight into how your actions may affect divorce proceedings and other matters, such as child custody, alimony, or property division. If the new person is truly deserving, they'll show understanding and be there once the divorce decree is finalized.

Day 69

Don't have sex with your soon-to-be ex-spouse.

Despite any temporary feelings of intimacy or nostalgia, such encounters often cloud judgment and hinder the process of moving forward with the divorce. It's essential to recognize that physical intimacy does not signify a reconciliation or resolution of underlying issues that led to the decision to divorce. Even if both parties agree to a casual encounter, it can create false hope or unrealistic expectations, ultimately prolonging the healing process.

Day 70

If you're determined to get your day in court so you can have justice for all the things your ex did wrong, you're likely throwing money away.

While it might feel tempting to air grievances and secure vindication for a sense of closure in court, it often comes at a significant financial cost. In the courtroom, it's all about facts, not feelings, so keep things strictly business in front of the judge. The judge will view your case from a business-like perspective, and it would be wise to do the same. Emotionally charged litigation can quickly escalate into a lengthy and expensive process, consuming resources you could use for building your post-divorce future. Instead of fixating on vengeance, focus on the future, free from negativity and chaos.

Chapter 3
It Takes a Village:
Assembling Your Team

Day 71

Don't rush to hire the first divorce lawyer you come across or the pit bull of a lawyer that a friend used.

When selecting a divorce lawyer, impulsive decisions can have lasting consequences. Resist the urge to hire the first attorney you find or opt for a notoriously aggressive lawyer based on someone else's recommendation. Instead, take the time to conduct thorough research for a lawyer who not only has the expertise but also aligns with your approach and values. Consider factors, such as communication style, negotiation tactics, and willingness to pursue amicable resolutions.

Day 72

*Find an attorney who supports your goals,
including setting the right tone.*

Look for an attorney who understands your priorities and
actively advocates for your best interests while also fostering a
collaborative and respectful atmosphere. This person should
support your goals, share your vision for an amicable
resolution, set the tone for productive negotiations, and
minimize unnecessary conflict. A skilled attorney can offer
valuable guidance and strategic advice, and advocate on your
behalf, empowering you to navigate the complexities of divorce
with confidence and clarity.

Day 73

*Moral support should come from loved ones, legal
advice must only be obtained from legal experts.*

While friends and family may offer well-intentioned advice
based on their own experiences, divorce laws and regulations
vary widely by jurisdiction and can be complex. Seeking legal
advice from a knowledgeable attorney ensures you receive
correct information about your rights, options, and potential
outcomes. Let family and friends provide emotional support,
but leave the legal advice to the experts!

Day 74

Establish a budget before choosing a lawyer.

Before starting attorney consultations, take the time to assess your financial situation and decide on a realistic budget for legal fees. Consider factors, such as hourly rates, retainer fees, and potential expenses for court appearances or mediation sessions. Discussing your budgetary considerations with prospective lawyers during the first consultations can help ensure transparency and prevent any surprises down the line.

Day 75

Keep searching until you find a lawyer who shares your goals but also feels like the perfect match for you.

Start by seeking recommendations from trusted sources, such as family and friends. Their experiences or referrals can offer valuable insights into lawyers who have effectively navigated similar situations. Consider getting recommendations from professionals within your network, such as therapists, financial advisors, or other legal professionals, who may offer valuable referrals based on their expertise and knowledge of your specific needs. Once you have a list, take the time to research each lawyer's qualifications, experience, and approach to divorce cases. Schedule consultations to assess compatibility. Don't settle until you find the one who meets your needs and expectations.

Day 76

Pit bull attorneys can often set an aggressive tone for negotiations, interfere with the settlement, and drive-up legal fees.

While it may be tempting to hire an aggressive attorney who fiercely advocates for your interests in divorce proceedings, it's essential to consider the potential drawbacks. Aggressive legal representatives can inadvertently escalate conflicts, set a hostile tone for negotiations, and hinder the settlement process. By prioritizing threatening tactics over cooperation and compromise, some attorneys may prolong litigation, exacerbate tensions between parties, and ultimately drive-up legal fees. Opting for a lawyer who prioritizes collaboration and looks to minimize conflict can lead to more efficient, cost-effective, and satisfactory outcomes.

Day 77

Ignore advice from people who tell you what to do.

True allies are the ones who bolster your confidence in making decisions aligned with your values and intuition. Their encouragement serves as a beacon of clarity amidst chaos, urging you to trust your instincts and prioritize your well-being. Surround yourself with individuals who uplift and support your journey, rather than those who look to impose their own agendas.

Day 78

Find a board-certified lawyer in marital and family law.

Sure, any lawyer could handle your divorce, but lawyers who are board-certified in marital and family law offer many advantages. These attorneys have undergone added education and training focused specifically on separation and divorce law, equipping them with the expertise and skills necessary to navigate even the most complex situations. By choosing a board-certified lawyer, you gain assurance that they possess a deep understanding of the intricacies of divorce law and are well-prepared to handle any challenges that may arise.

Day 79

The more money you spend on legal fees, the less you'll have to begin your new life. This is not to say you should skimp; just be aware.

It's important to keep in mind that every dollar spent on legal fees during divorce proceedings is a dollar that you could invest in building your new life post-divorce. While it's crucial not to skimp on quality legal representation, it's equally important to stay mindful of your budget and expenditure. If fees are getting out of control during the process, have an honest conversation with your attorney to decide how to get back on track.

Day 80

First, decide what type of divorce you want. Then, hire the right type of legal professional to support you.

It's essential to first determine the type of divorce process that aligns with your needs and preferences. Whether it's arbitration, litigation, collaborative divorce, or summary or contested divorce, each approach offers distinct advantages and considerations. Once you've identified the type of divorce you want, selecting the right lawyer becomes paramount. Look for a legal professional who specializes in your chosen approach and has a proven history of success in guiding clients through similar circumstances.

You and your soon-to-be ex-spouse may not see eye-to-eye on the type of divorce you want. This initial negotiation is crucial. By staying open in communication and expressing a mutual desire for respectful progress, there's a chance to find common ground and opt for a smoother, less adversarial process.

Day 81

*Create a personal board of directors filled with
wise friends and mentors.*

A personal board of directors made up of trusted friends and mentors can provide invaluable support and guidance. Whether offering a listening ear or emotional support or giving practical advice, each member of your personal board brings a unique perspective to the table. Their collective wisdom and guidance can help you make informed decisions, maintain perspective, and cultivate resilience throughout the process. Just remember to leave legal advice to your lawyer!

Day 82

*Be selective about what you share and with whom.
Keep your circle of trust small!*

It's crucial to maintain confidentiality and trust throughout the divorce process, as sharing sensitive details with too many people can complicate matters and escalate tensions. Conflicting opinions and advice will often confuse your decision-making ability. Keep your circle of trust small, confiding only in those who have your best interests at heart and can offer constructive support. Remember, each conversation carries weight, so choose wisely and prioritize keeping a sense of confidentiality and trust.

Day 83

*Make sure you have three friends: the Comedian,
the Rock, and the Resource.*

The Comedian brings levity and humor to difficult situations, offering moments of respite and laughter amidst the challenges. The Rock serves as a pillar of strength and stability, offering unwavering support and a listening ear when needed most. The Resource is a wealth of knowledge and guidance, offering practical advice and information to help you make informed decisions. These friends form a valuable support system, not only throughout your divorce but for a lifetime.

Day 84

*You need at least one friend who
understands what you do not say.*

Having a friend who understands us with no words is invaluable. They offer unwavering support and empathy, intuitively grasping our unspoken thoughts and emotions. This friend serves as a compassionate listener and a comforting presence, providing solace and validation during times of struggle. It's so nice to have a friend who you can go for a walk with and not say a word, but through their presence, know that they love and support you. Through their understanding of your journey, they offer a lifeline of support, reminding you that you are not alone in your experience.

Day 85

If you want your divorce to be painless, find a committed attorney to help keep your divorce civil while also protecting your rights and interests.

Let's be realistic ... no divorce is painless, but with the right team, you can minimize the discomfort. Seek dedicated legal counsel to foster an amicable resolution and minimize conflict. Look for someone who values collaboration over confrontation and will find mutually beneficial solutions that prioritize the well-being of both spouses and children. By partnering with an attorney who shares your goal of a civil divorce, you can navigate the process with greater ease and dignity.

Day 86

Get clear on your lawyer's fee structure upfront.

It's essential to clarify the specifics of your lawyer's fee structure before you sign on with them to avoid surprises later. Ask the attorney about potential added costs that could be incurred throughout the process, such as court filing fees, administrative expenses, or charges for extra services. By gaining clarity on the fee structure from the outset, you can make informed decisions about your legal representation and budget accordingly. Additionally, discussing fees in advance helps establish transparency and ensures that you and your attorney are on the same page about financial expectations.

Day 87

*Listen to your legal team, but be prepared
to make your own decisions.*

Your divorce professional, whether a lawyer, mediator, or counselor, can offer valuable insight and guidance based on their ability and experience. However, you know your situation, priorities, and goals best. Trust your instincts when making decisions, as they are ultimately the ones that will impact your future. By taking an active role in the decision-making process, you can ensure that your divorce aligns with your needs and aspirations.

Day 88

*If assets are straightforward, your accountant may
provide support and direction for the near term.*

General accountants have expertise in financial matters and can help assess the value of assets, such as bank accounts, investments, and retirement accounts, and provide guidance on dividing them fairly. They can also help navigate tax implications associated with asset division and ensure compliance with financial regulations. While more complex divorces often require the expertise of a financial planner or forensic accountant, an accountant may be able to effectively manage simpler cases.

Day 89

If assets are sizeable or complex, you may benefit from a Certified Divorce Financial Analyst.

In cases where assets are substantial and intricate, enlisting the expertise of a Certified Divorce Financial Analyst (CDFA) can prove invaluable. A CDFA can help assess the value of complex assets, such as businesses, investments, and real estate holdings, ensuring that all assets are accurately valued and accounted for during the divorce process. Additionally, a CDFA can provide guidance on tax implications associated with asset division and help address issues related to pension and retirement plans.

Day 90

Support from a financial planner can be helpful to plan for future goals.

While your accountant is good for today's issues, a financial planner can help you assess your future financial situation and formulate a strategic plan for achieving long-term goals post-divorce. They can offer insight into budgeting, saving, investing, retirement planning, and managing assets to ensure financial stability and security. By collaborating with a financial planner, you can develop a personalized financial roadmap tailored to your unique circumstances.

Day 91

A divorce therapist can be an important resource.

As you navigate the emotional rollercoaster of divorce, seeking support from a therapist specially trained to assist individuals through divorce can be very helpful. A trained therapist provides a safe and non-judgmental space for you to explore your feelings, process your emotions, and develop coping strategies. This goes for children too. A child divorce counselor is a licensed psychologist, counselor, social worker, or therapist trained to offer support to children experiencing a divorce.

Day 92

Read up, talk to only level-headed people who have been in your shoes, and consider a divorce counselor.

Educating yourself about divorce laws and procedures, empowers you to make informed decisions. Speaking with level-headed individuals who have firsthand experience with divorce can offer practical insight, emotional support, and perspective. Their empathy and understanding can offer comfort and reassurance. Additionally, seeking guidance from a divorce counselor or therapist can provide a safe space to express emotions, process feelings, and develop coping strategies to manage stress and anxiety. By combining these resources, you can gain clarity, perspective, and resilience.

Day 93

*Be selective about which online groups
you join or resources you use.*

There is an overwhelming number of online resources available to provide support and guidance for those navigating divorce. However, it's important to be careful about which groups or resources to engage with, as not all may offer reliable or relevant information. Ask your lawyer or therapist for recommendations. Some groups can easily become a negative space for complaining. If the group is not a positive, encouraging space, simply back away and find a group that supports your approach.

Day 94

A good therapist can help manage emotions.

A therapist offers a safe and non-judgmental space to process feelings of grief, anger, confusion, and anxiety, helping you to untangle the emotional knots and find clarity amidst the chaos. Through therapy, you can develop coping strategies, gain insights into your thought patterns and behaviors, and learn effective communication skills to navigate the challenges of co-parenting and rebuilding your life post-divorce. Many times, the issues and emotions you experience during divorce stem from past experiences.

Day 95

Be careful who you trust. Sugar and salt look the same.

The decision of whom to trust carries profound significance, reminiscent of distinguishing between sugar and salt. Individuals may present themselves with equal charm and warmth, masking their true intentions beneath a façade of sincerity. Yet, just as a discerning palate can detect the subtle differences between sugar's sweetness and salt's sour essence, one must also exercise caution in discerning the authenticity of those they invite into their inner circle. Trust, once given, is a delicate thread that weaves the fabric of connection and vulnerability. However, misplaced trust can yield bitter consequences.

Day 96

Get to the root of grievances, shame, and anger.

Anger and shame will continue to chip away at happiness if not managed properly. By working with a therapist, you can explore the root causes of these emotions, identify patterns of thinking and behavior, and develop healthy coping strategies. Therapy offers a safe space where you can express yourself openly and receive guidance and support from a trained professional. The self-work you do during this time will be invaluable in the years ahead.

Day 97

Learn how to lower your emotional reactivity.

Learning how to lower your emotional reactivity can help you respond to difficult situations with grace, clarity, and resilience. Practices, such as mindfulness, deep breathing exercises, and cognitive-behavioral techniques, can help you regulate your emotions and cultivate a sense of inner calm. When faced with unexpected challenges, you will be better equipped to pause and respond, versus having a knee-jerk reaction which could have unintended consequences.

Day 98

Take everyone's advice with a grain of salt.

While it's important to listen to others' perspectives, it's equally important to take everyone's advice with a grain of salt. Every divorce is unique, and what worked for someone else may not apply to your situation. Consider the source of the advice, their experiences, and how it aligns with your values and circumstances. Ultimately, trust your instincts and make decisions that feel right for you and your family. Seeking professional guidance from a divorce attorney or counselor can also give tailored advice and support based on your specific needs and goals.

Day 99

Do you want short-term revenge or long-term peace?

It's completely normal to want someone who will fiercely fight in your corner, but pause for a moment and reflect on your motivations. Are you seeking immediate retribution or long-lasting serenity? While it's tempting to opt for the former, remember that the aftermath of divorce can be a lengthy journey, one where bitterness and resentment might only prolong the healing process. A super-aggressive lawyer may win battles in the short term, but what about the long-term war for your future happiness? Striking a balance between advocating for your rights and fostering an amicable resolution is key. Divorce isn't just a legal process; it's a personal one too. Your choices today will shape your tomorrow.

Day 100

Mediation lessens miscommunication.

With mediation, couples engage in communication facilitated by a neutral third-party mediator. This minimizes the likelihood of misunderstandings that often arise in more adversarial legal proceedings. By engaging in open and honest dialogue during mediation sessions, you can work together to find mutually beneficial solutions and reach agreements that address your unique needs and concerns.

Day 101

*Look for and accept support from friends,
clergy, and professional counselors.*

Friends and family members who offer a listening ear and
words of encouragement can provide much-needed emotional
support, reminding you that you're not alone in your struggles.
Clergy members or spiritual advisors can also offer spiritual
guidance and a sense of solace, helping you find meaning and
strength in your faith or beliefs. Professional counselors or
therapists specializing in divorce can provide support, offering
strategies to cope with emotions, navigate co-parenting
challenges, and make informed decisions about your future.
You may benefit from many types of support throughout the
divorce process. Tap into the resources needed for the specific
challenge you're facing and realize you can change to someone
or something that works better for your ever-fluctuating
situation at any time.

Day 102

It's your life and you get to choose who you invite in.

It's your life, and you hold the power to decide who and what you allow into it. This isn't just about physical spaces or social circles; it's about safeguarding your emotional and mental well-being. During this challenging time, take stock of the relationships and influences that surround you. Are they uplifting and supportive, or do they drain your energy and perpetuate negativity? Recognize that you have the power to curate your inner circle, filling it with individuals who genuinely uplift and empower you. Next, consider the thoughts and beliefs that occupy your mind. Are they serving your growth and healing, or are they holding you back in bitterness and resentment? Embrace the power of self-awareness and self-compassion, consciously choosing thoughts and perspectives that align with your journey toward peace and self-discovery.

Chapter 4
From Shared to Separate: Navigating the Division of Assets

Day 103

Don't get bogged down with the unimportant things, like who gets the big TV.

Arguments over material possessions can distract us from more pressing issues and prolong the process. Instead of fixating on these insignificant details, it's important to maintain perspective and focus on what truly matters for your future well-being. By letting go of your attachment to material items and avoiding unnecessary conflict, you can streamline the divorce process and move forward with clarity and peace of mind. Ultimately, prioritizing your emotional health and long-term happiness is far more valuable than any possession.

Day 104

If you want to stay in the house, consider every single detail, financial and otherwise.

While the idea of staying in the marital house may hold sentimental value or provide a sense of stability, it's essential to assess whether it's a feasible option. Consider the financial implications, such as mortgage payments, property taxes, utilities, and maintenance costs, and decide whether you can afford to cover these expenses independently. You'll also need to factor in the time it will take to maintain the house. Do you want to begin your next chapter by spending your free time cutting the grass, shoveling snow, or fixing the pipes?

Day 105

Treat divorce negotiations like a business transaction.

By adopting a pragmatic mindset, you can focus on finding practical solutions. Approach discussions with objectivity and professionalism, prioritizing clear communication and mutual respect. Just as in business dealings, it's crucial to manage your emotions and maintain a goal-oriented perspective during negotiations. Your former spouse might try to provoke a reaction, so take a moment to consider whether the item in question is truly important to you or if you're motivated by a desire to withhold it from them.

Day 106

Be realistic and don't feel entitled to the same lifestyle.

While it's natural to desire continuity and comfort, divorce often requires adjustments to your standard of living. Instead of clinging to entitlement or unrealistic expectations, approach the situation with realism and flexibility. Assess your financial situation objectively and prioritize your long-term stability and well-being over keeping the same lifestyle. This may involve downsizing, budgeting more carefully, or reevaluating spending habits to align with your new circumstances. Compromise may be short-term, too. Once you get back on your feet, then you can reevaluate which parts of your former life you can afford.

Day 107

Don't get mired down in things that don't matter.

It is so easy to get bogged down in trivial details and petty disagreements. However, you must keep your focus on the bigger picture. By refusing to get caught up in insignificant matters, you can allocate your time, energy, and resources toward what truly matters: your well-being, your future, and the welfare of your family. A great goal to have during divorce is to navigate the process with dignity, respect, and fairness, ensuring a smooth transition into the next chapter of your life.

Day 108

Act on your goals, not your emotions.

Acting on goals rather than emotions means taking a step back to assess the situation objectively, considering long-term implications, and making decisions that align with your values and what you want for your life. This approach may involve seeking advice from trusted friends, family members, or professionals who can offer a balanced perspective and help you weigh the pros and cons of different options. By focusing on your goals, whether they involve financial stability, co-parenting arrangements, or personal well-being, you can make decisions that serve your best interests in the long run, rather than reacting impulsively to immediate emotions.

Day 109

The more you and your spouse can negotiate your settlement, the more time and money you will save.

Cooperative discussions allow you to address key issues, such as asset division and child custody in a way that reflects your circumstances and priorities. By reaching agreements outside of court, you keep greater control over the outcome of your divorce and are better positioned to remain amicable. By investing time and effort into constructive dialogue, you pave the way for a more peaceful divorce experience, letting both of you move forward with greater ease and financial stability.

Day 110

Decide what is most important to you, then write it down, create a plan, and work on it every day.

Take a moment to think about what you want to achieve in the divorce and in life, then write it down. Putting your goals on paper helps you focus and gives you a plan to follow. Once you have a clear plan, try to do something small every day to get closer to your goals. Having a plan in place will also help you make important decisions quickly when needed. You can look at your long-term goals and choose what's best for them. Whether it's taking care of yourself, dealing with legal stuff, or handling tough emotions, sticking to your plan is important.

Day 111

Get clear on your negotiables, so you don't end up feeling disempowered and unable to move forward.

Without a clear understanding of your non-negotiable priorities and areas open to negotiation, you risk feeling overwhelmed and disempowered by the complexities of the process. Take the time to identify your essential needs, such as financial security, co-parenting arrangements, and emotional well-being, as well as areas where you are willing to compromise. For example, you may place more importance on having cash in hand, versus the retirement account.

Day 112

*Seeing the bigger picture makes it easier
to accept certain compromises.*

While certain compromises may be challenging to accept in the short-term, recognizing their significance within the larger context of achieving greater stability, well-being, and peace of mind can provide a sense of perspective and clarity. Embracing a forward-thinking mindset can empower you to focus on the outcomes that matter most to you, fostering resilience and adaptability in the face of challenges.

Day 113

*Don't promise when you're happy, don't reply when
you're angry, and don't decide when you're sad.*

Avoid impulsively making promises during moments of happiness, as they may not align with your long-term interests. Refrain from responding to communications when anger clouds your judgment, as reactive responses can escalate conflict and hinder productive dialogue. When experiencing sadness or emotional distress, avoid making major decisions, as temporary feelings rather than rational thinking may influence them. Instead, allow yourself time to process your emotions and regain clarity before making any significant commitments or choices.

Day 114

Don't be stubborn or hard-headed.

Try to avoid digging your heels in or being too set in your ways. It's essential to remain open-minded and flexible, especially during the divorce process. Holding onto stubbornness can prolong conflicts and hinder progress toward resolution. Instead, consider the bigger picture and prioritize finding common ground. By being willing to compromise and adapt, you pave the way for smoother negotiations and a more amicable separation. Divorce is already a challenging time, and being overly rigid can add unnecessary stress.

Day 115

Be prepared to compromise.

Holding onto rigid demands can escalate conflicts and prolong the process. Instead, approach negotiations with an open mind and a willingness to find common ground. Consider what aspects of the settlement are most important to you and be ready to make concessions in other areas. Remember, compromise is not a sign of weakness, but a pragmatic approach to resolving differences and finding a mutually satisfactory outcome. By embracing compromise, you can facilitate more productive discussions and foster a cooperative atmosphere, ultimately paving the way for a smoother transition to post-divorce life.

Day 116

Revenge is a total waste of time.

Think about the future impact of getting caught up in retaliatory actions and instead, focus on promoting understanding and reconciliation. Choosing forgiveness, empathy, and compassion can interrupt the pattern of retaliation, leading to healing and resolution. Consider whether staying in a cycle of emotional conflict is worth it or if stepping back and refusing to take part in unproductive behavior is more beneficial. Opting to move beyond the urge for revenge and striving for agreement through peaceful methods allows you to handle divorce with dignity and poise.

Day 117

Choose your battles wisely.

Not all battles are worth fighting, and spending energy on trivial matters can detract from addressing more significant issues. By prioritizing your battles, you can focus on resolving conflicts that truly matter and have a meaningful impact on your life post-divorce. By taking this strategy, you will conserve your emotional and mental resources, keep your sanity amidst the chaos, and manage the divorce process more effectively. Remember, the goal isn't to win every skirmish but to secure a fair resolution that allows you to move forward with peace of mind.

Day 118

When times get tough, repeat, "This too shall pass."

This simple yet powerful phrase serves as a beacon of hope and reassurance during times of distress and uncertainty. By acknowledging that the challenges you face are temporary and that brighter days lie ahead, you cultivate resilience and fortitude to weather the storm. When overwhelmed by emotions or facing tough decisions, repeating this mantra offers a moment of clarity and perspective, reminding you to persevere with patience and strength.

Day 119

You can agree to co-own the home with a deferred sale.

In divorce settlements, the marital home often becomes a focal point of negotiation because of its significant value. One approach is to agree to maintain co-ownership of the property mutually and sell it at a later time. This arrangement could be beneficial if you aim to provide stability for your children by keeping them in the same school district until they finish their education. However, it's important to recognize that this decision prolongs your ties to your ex-spouse. While it may initially seem appealing, it's crucial to carefully consider the implications before committing. Take the time to evaluate the long-term effects and assess whether this option aligns with your future goals and aspirations.

Day 120

*Is what you are doing today getting you closer
to where you want to be tomorrow?*

Every decision made in the present carries the potential to shape the trajectory of your future. By introspectively evaluating the choices and behaviors of today, you can decide whether you are moving closer to your desired destination or veering off course. This self-inquiry prompts reflection on whether current actions contribute to healing, self-improvement, and the pursuit of personal goals. It encourages you to prioritize activities that nurture your well-being, cultivate resilience, and foster a sense of purpose.

Chapter 5
Words Matter:
Respectful Communication
During Tough Times

Day 121

Don't raise your voice; improve your argument.

Rather than engaging in yelling matches or confrontations, focus on refining your arguments and expressing your points clearly. Strengthening the quality of your arguments allows you to communicate your viewpoints with clarity, reason, and compassion, fostering empathy and cooperation with your soon-to-be ex-partner. Approach challenging discussions from a factual standpoint rather than reacting emotionally. This method not only encourages respectful and constructive conversation but also increases the chances of reaching mutually helpful resolutions. By prioritizing effective communication and rational discourse, you can navigate the divorce process with greater understanding and civility, creating a harmonious post-divorce relationship.

Day 122

*For divorce to be as painless as possible,
set aside who's right and wrong.*

By rationally approaching negotiations, divorcing couples can find common ground, prioritize their interests, and work toward mutually beneficial solutions. This pragmatic approach allows you to move beyond the emotional complexities of divorce and make decisions based on practical considerations, such as financial stability, co-parenting arrangements, and your future well-being. If you find yourself focused on who's right and who's wrong, work with a therapist to get to the root of why this is so important to you and if this means more to you than moving on to the next chapter.

Day 123

*When asked a question you don't want to answer, smile
and say, "That's not something I can share."*

Some people will genuinely care about you, while others may fish for gossip. Be discerning with what information you share. Imagine this: you keep a composed demeanor, offering a courteous smile while calmly stating, "That's not something I can share." This approach tactfully communicates your boundaries without ending the conversation or divulging more than you should.

Day 124

*Think before you speak. There is no
delete key for the spoken word.*

While written words offer the luxury of revision or deletion, spoken words pack a hefty punch, often leaving enduring impressions. It's crucial to pause and reflect on the potential impact of your words, as they can either sidestep misunderstandings and conflicts or amplify them. Carefully selecting your words ensures they convey your thoughts and emotions clearly, empathetically, and respectfully. Quick retorts laden with hurt can lead to significant time spent mending wounds, diverting attention from crucial discussions.

Day 125

Everyone fights; it's how you do it that matters.

While disagreements may arise, approaching conflicts with empathy, patience, and constructive communication can make all the difference. It's essential to recognize that how you manage conflict can have a profound impact on the overall dynamics of the divorce process and the well-being of everyone involved. By approaching disagreements with empathy and integrity, you create a positive and cooperative environment, ultimately leading to smoother negotiations and a more amicable resolution of their differences.

Day 126

If you have nothing nice to say, stay silent.

This wise advice underscores the importance of thoughtful communication and restraint, especially during times of heightened emotions and tensions. It's crucial to pause and reflect before speaking, considering the potential impact of your words. Choosing silence over impulsivity allows for the preservation of peace and the prevention of unnecessary conflict. You can always respond neutrally by saying, "I'm not in a place to discuss that topic right now." It also offers an opportunity for introspection and self-control, enabling you to move forward with greater composure and maturity.

Day 127

Don't make knee-jerk decisions or allow arguments to escalate into screaming matches.

Emotions will run high, but reacting impulsively can increase tension and complicate matters. Instead, work hard to keep a calm and rational approach to communication and decision-making. Take the time to weigh your options, seek advice from trusted advisors, and consider the potential consequences of your actions. Patience, diplomacy, and level-headedness are key to navigating the complexities of divorce with dignity and respect.

Day 128

*If something is intense and uncomfortable, be ready to
say, "I understand you need to address this topic, but
I need a bit more time before I'm ready."*

If a topic feels overwhelming, it's okay to acknowledge its
importance while expressing the need for more time to process
your thoughts before engaging in further conversation. By
articulating your boundaries and advocating for yourself, you
assert control over the pace and direction of discussions,
making sure they occur in a way that feels manageable and
respectful to you. It is, however, important to schedule a date
to resume the conversation so the delay does not come across
as though you are trying to sidestep the topic.

Day 129

Don't let a crappy situation bring out the worst in you.

Resist the temptation to succumb to negativity and allow
difficult circumstances to dictate your behavior. Instead, strive
to keep a positive outlook and inner strength. By focusing on
the opportunities for growth and renewal that divorce
presents, rather than dwelling on the hardships, you empower
yourself to rise above adversity and emerge stronger.
Cultivating positivity not only helps your well-being, but also
sets a constructive example for those around you, including
children.

Day 130

Don't keep score.

Amid divorce, it's easy to fall into the trap of keeping score, tallying perceived slights or grievances as if they were points on a scoreboard. However, this approach only breeds resentment and prolongs conflict. Instead, focus on finding common ground and solutions that prioritize mutual respect and cooperation. Remember, divorce is not about winning or losing, but about finding fair resolutions that allow both parties to transition to the next phase of their lives with dignity and respect.

Day 131

Don't let anyone guilt you.

It's natural for friends, family members, or even your ex-partner to try to sway your decisions or make you feel guilty about the choices you're making. It's important to remember that you are the one who knows what's best for yourself and your future. Having a neutral, pre-scripted response can help you respond to the situation. One example is, "I hear you, and I appreciate your perspective. However, I need to prioritize what's best for me." Trust your instincts and stand firm in your decisions, regardless of outside opinions or attempts to manipulate you emotionally.

Day 132

Don't approach a divorce like a boxing match, but as an opportunity to thank each other for the good times and for the love you shared for each other at some point.

It will be tough, but embracing a mindset of appreciation and acknowledgment can foster a more respectful and amicable divorce process. By recognizing and honoring the good times and the love that once existed between you and your soon-to-be ex-spouse, you can approach divorce with empathy, compassion, and mutual respect. Expressing gratitude for the positive aspects of your relationship can help ease animosity and promote healing, allowing you both to navigate the divorce journey with greater grace and understanding.

Day 133

Mutual respect and compromise will allow you both to maintain privacy and escape divorce with less drama.

By respecting each other's boundaries and privacy, you can navigate the divorce process with greater dignity and less emotional strain. This means refraining from engaging in behaviors that could escalate tensions, such as airing grievances publicly or trying to sabotage each other's reputations. Focus on finding common ground and reaching agreements that prioritize the well-being of all involved, including children.

Day 134

Yelling and screaming never solves a thing.

There will be times during the divorce process when emotions run high and tension goes through the roof. Resorting to combative behaviors only intensifies conflict and undermines productive communication. Effective communication is key to navigating the complexities of divorce, and it requires patience, empathy, and restraint. By keeping a calm and respectful demeanor, you will create an open environment for constructive dialogue and negotiation. If you feel like the conversation is about to turn into a scream-fest, it is best to pause and continue the conversation later.

Day 135

Look the person in the eyes when you say, "I'm sorry."

When uttering the words, "I'm sorry," it's essential to accompany them with genuine eye contact, as this gesture signifies sincerity and respect. Eye contact conveys empathy and authenticity, allowing the other person to feel acknowledged and validated in their emotions. By making direct eye contact when offering an apology, you also show a willingness to take accountability for any hurt or harm caused. This simple yet powerful act can help mend fractured relationships and pave the way for healing and closure.

Day 136

"We have two ears and one mouth so that you can listen twice as much as you speak." —*Epictetus*

Instead of letting emotions steer the conversation or jumping in with your own opinions right away, try taking a moment to pause and genuinely listen to the other person. It's easy to get caught up in planning our response, but that often means we miss out on understanding the other side. By practicing patient and empathetic listening, you can lay the groundwork for mutual respect, trust, and cooperation. These qualities are crucial for gracefully navigating the intricate terrain of divorce with dignity and compassion.

Day 137

Ask yourself, do you want to be right or happy?

Constantly striving to prove your point in an argument can drain valuable energy and prolong the emotional turmoil of the divorce process. Instead of fixating on being right, it's essential to prioritize personal well-being and emotional health. This means asking yourself a fundamental question: do I want to be happy or right? Choosing happiness over the need to prove yourself right can lead to greater peace of mind and emotional resilience. It involves letting go of the desire to win arguments and focusing on fostering positive relationships, maintaining self-respect, and nurturing personal growth.

Day 138

Avoid fights about the past. Troubles and wrongs are all things that you can hash out with a therapist, not your soon-to-be ex-spouse.

While it's natural to want to address unresolved issues, doing so in divorce proceedings often leads to further conflict and animosity. Instead, seek support from a therapist or counselor to process and work through your emotions constructively. When you refrain from bringing up past grievances during divorce negotiations, you will foster an amicable and productive atmosphere, allowing for smoother resolution of issues and a healthier transition into post-divorce life.

Day 139

"To be wronged is nothing unless you continue to remember it." — Confucius

Clinging to resentment and grievances only prolongs suffering and impedes the healing process. By releasing the weight of past hurts and injustices, you can liberate yourself from the burden of resentment and create space for healing and growth. Instead of dwelling on past wrongs, intentionally choose to cultivate forgiveness, understanding, and compassion for both you and your former spouse. This may be the last thing you want to do, but remember, you're doing it for your own healing, peace, and closure.

Day 140

Knowing how your soon-to-be ex deals with conflict will allow you to better prepare.

By understanding your soon-to-be ex-spouse's conflict management style, you can expect their responses and tailor your approach, leading to productive and successful negotiations. Rather than relying on wishful thinking or unrealistic expectations, basing your strategies on the reality of your ex-partner's behavior allows for informed decision-making and clearer communication. Remember, nothing good will come from remaining passive.

Day 141

Commit to having mutual respect.

By valuing each other's perspectives, feelings, and autonomy, you can cultivate empathy and understanding, even in the face of adversity. This commitment to mutual respect lays the groundwork for healthier communication, cooperation, and conflict resolution, ultimately leading to positive outcomes for both of you. Fostering mutual respect also sets a positive example for the children involved, promoting their emotional well-being and helping them navigate the complexities of divorce with greater resilience and understanding. You don't have to agree with what is being said or done, but respect goes a long way toward a peaceful settlement.

Day 142

There are three sides to every argument:
side 1, side 2, and the truth.

Throughout your divorce, each party may vigorously advocate for their version of the truth. However, the reality often lies somewhere in between. Embracing the idea that there are three sides to every argument encourages humility, open-mindedness, and a willingness to seek common ground, ultimately facilitating more constructive and harmonious resolutions amid the challenges of divorce.

Day 143

Honesty always ... but not as a weapon
or to cause excessive hurt.

While honesty is paramount, wield it with sensitivity and discretion, using it as a tool to foster open dialogue rather than as a weapon to cause excessive hurt or harm. Honesty serves as a foundation for open dialogue and mutual understanding, allowing you to navigate the complexities of your separation with integrity and respect. However, it's essential to recognize the delicate balance between honesty and tact, ensuring that you convey the truth in a manner that is compassionate and considerate of the other person's feelings. Ultimately, honesty should serve as a tool for healing and reconciliation, rather than as a source of further pain or division.

Day 144

*If you must say something negative, say
two positive things as well.*

It's like the golden rule of communication—never let the negativity overshadow the good stuff. By throwing in a couple of positives, you're not just softening the blow, but also keeping the conversation on a positive track. Plus, it shows that you're not all about raining on someone's parade; you're willing to give credit where credit is due. Next time you're tempted to let out some steam, remember to sprinkle in a little positivity too.

Day 145

*Fights are not an acceptable form of communication.
Learn to talk things out.*

Divorce often arises from a communication breakdown, where conflicts escalate into harmful arguments and pain for both parties. Talking things out calmly and respectfully fosters understanding and empathy, leading to resolution and healing. Effective communication involves active listening, expressing feelings without blame, and looking to understand perspectives. By prioritizing healthy communication, you can work toward minimizing fights, building trust, and laying the groundwork for constructive co-parenting.

Day 146

Conflict is like pouring alcohol on a wound.

Like alcohol disinfecting a wound, conflict can address underlying issues, prevent further harm, and facilitate healing. While it may be uncomfortable and challenging to confront conflict head-on, avoiding it can allow the wound to fester and worsen. Addressing conflicts directly can lead to resolution, growth, and a sense of closure. It's about recognizing that conflict, though painful, can be a necessary step toward healing and moving forward after divorce.

Day 147

In an argument, start with what you have in common...
you may find you're closer to resolution than you think.

While disagreements may seem impossible to resolve, acknowledging shared values, goals, or experiences can serve as a foundation for constructive dialogue. By highlighting areas of agreement, you may discover common threads, despite the rifts caused by the dissolution of the relationship. This approach shifts the focus from divisiveness to unity, encouraging empathy and cooperation, rather than escalating conflict. Starting with common ground opens the door to productive communication, paving the way for mutual respect and potentially smoother negotiations.

Day 148

KMS (keep mouth shut) is the single piece of advice that can prevent an enormous amount of trouble.

This simple yet profound advice underscores the importance of thinking before speaking, especially in moments of heated emotion or impulse. By exercising self-control and refraining from voicing every thought or opinion, you can prevent misunderstandings, conflicts, and regrettable actions. Whether in personal relationships, professional settings, or everyday interactions, the practice of keeping one's mouth shut can diffuse tension, preserve harmony, and maintain dignity. It encourages thoughtful reflection and consideration of the potential consequences of words spoken in haste or anger.

Day 149

In disagreements, be fair. Don't bring old baggage.

It's natural for emotions to run high during an argument, but revisiting past hurts only escalates tensions and prolongs the healing process. Instead, work to address current issues with a focus on finding mutually beneficial solutions. By keeping the discussion centered on the present and avoiding the temptation to rehash past conflicts, you can foster a constructive and amicable dialogue. While it may be difficult to set aside past grievances, doing so is essential to keep the conversation and resolution moving forward.

Day 150

In disagreements, never lose the lesson.

When tensions rise, it's easy to become consumed by emotions, but each disagreement presents an opportunity for personal growth and insight. Rather than allowing conflicts to spiral into negativity, approach them with an open mind and a willingness to learn. By delving into the underlying causes of disagreements, you can gain a deeper understanding of yourself, fostering personal development and emotional resilience.

Day 151

It is better to tell a hurtful truth than a comforting lie.

Divorce can be a minefield of emotions, but in navigating those tough conversations, honesty truly is the best policy. It might sting a bit to hear the truth, but in the long run, it's far better than comforting someone with a lie. Being upfront and honest with your soon-to-be ex-spouse not only fosters trust and respect but also lays the foundation for healthier communication. This holds true when you receive a hurtful truth. Take a deep breath and receive the information, knowing it may sting, but it is better than someone feeding you lies. It's all about facing the reality of the situation head-on, even if it's uncomfortable.

Day 152

Don't continue to argue just to prove you're right.

When the storm clouds of disagreement roll in, it's essential to keep your cool, especially during a divorce. Remember, the goal isn't to win the argument at all costs, but to find common ground and reach a resolution that works for both parties. So, take a deep breath, count to ten if you must, and resist the urge to prolong the argument just to prove a point. It can be tempting to dig in your heels and fight tooth and nail, but ultimately, it's not about being right—it's about finding a way forward that respects you both.

Day 153

Your life is mostly shaped by your reactions.

Instead of succumbing to bitterness or despair, you can choose resilience and optimism. It's within your reaction where the real transformation occurs. By adopting an initiative-taking mindset, you can turn adversity into opportunity, using the challenges of divorce as a catalyst for personal growth and self-discovery. Whether it's finding new passions, strengthening relationships with loved ones, or embarking on new adventures, the way you choose to respond to life's trials shapes your character and determines your happiness.

Day 154

Be kind to unkind people; they need it the most.

Now is the most important time to remember the power of kindness, even toward those who may have contributed to the pain. Divorce often involves complex emotions, including hurt, anger, and resentment, which can lead to unkind behavior from both parties. However, responding with kindness, even in the face of animosity, can help diffuse tension and foster healing for everyone involved. While it may be challenging to extend kindness to someone who has caused pain, it's important to recognize that their animosity may stem from their own struggles, insecurities, or past experiences.

Day 155

The blame game is a two-way street.

It's natural to feel hurt, angry, and inclined to place blame on the other party for the breakdown of the relationship. However, it's crucial to recognize that assigning blame to the other person is often counterproductive. Blaming the other person without acknowledging one's own role in the relationship's challenges can hinder personal growth and healing. Instead of focusing on assigning blame, reflect on your actions, behaviors, and contributions to the relationship's dynamic.

Day 156

*Have a standard response ready as the reason for the
divorce that doesn't cause shame or embarrassment
for you, your former spouse, or your kids.*

During a divorce, it's helpful to have a pre-planned answer
ready for when people ask about the reason for the separation.
You should craft the response in a way that avoids assigning
blame or causing embarrassment to any party involved. This
will help keep you and your soon-to-be ex-spouse's dignity and
respect, while also preserving privacy and minimizing gossip
or speculation from others.

Day 157

Never say anything deliberately cruel.

In the emotionally charged atmosphere of divorce, it's crucial
to remember the power of words and the lasting impact they
can have. While disagreements will arise, deliberately inflicting
pain with cruel words only inflames the already difficult
situation. Words spoken in anger or spite can linger in the
minds and hearts of both parties long after the divorce
proceedings are over, causing deep wounds that may take years
to heal. Instead, communicating with kindness, empathy, and
respect, even during disagreements, can help minimize further
harm and foster an amicable resolution

Divorce Mess to Happiness

Day 158

Be a bee spreading honey, not a fly spreading poo.

Emotions are going to run high, and it's easy to get caught up in negativity and conflict. However, the analogy of being a bee spreading honey rather than a fly spreading poo serves as a powerful reminder to choose positivity and kindness, especially during challenging times. Instead of worsening tensions and spreading negativity crap, strive to spread sweetness and warmth through your words and actions.

Day 159

Be kind whenever possible.

Despite the emotional upheaval and discord that may go with the dissolution of a marriage, choosing kindness remains a steadfast compass guiding the way forward. It's a gentle reminder that even in moments of pain and uncertainty, compassion has the power to mend wounds and soothe aching hearts. It's a simple yet profound truth: kindness is not contingent on circumstance; it thrives in every moment, inviting us to embrace its transformative power. So, in the hectic journey of divorce, remember to be kind whenever possible. And the beautiful truth? It's always possible.

Day 160

Admit when you're wrong.

Admitting when you're wrong fosters humility and shows maturity, both of which are invaluable qualities during the divorce process. It allows for open dialogue and eases the resolution of conflicts, paving the way for smoother negotiations and compromises. In addition, acknowledging your mistakes can lead to greater self-awareness and introspection, enabling you to learn from past experiences and avoid repeating similar errors in the future.

Day 161

*Lowering your voice when angry works
just as well as raising it.*

Lowering your voice when you're upset is a powerful technique that can diffuse tension and promote productive communication. When you speak softly, it forces both you and your ex-partner to lean in and listen attentively, fostering a sense of familiarity and understanding. It also signals to the other person that you are in control of your emotions and are committed to resolving the issue peacefully. Speaking in a calm tone can also help de-escalate the situation, preventing it from spiraling into a full-blown argument.

Day 162

Never say, "I told you so."

Recognize that everyone makes mistakes, and pointing fingers only deepens wounds and prolongs healing. By refraining from saying, "I told you so," you show maturity and compassion, acknowledging that your ex-partner's decisions, though perhaps misguided, were made with the best intentions. By choosing not to gloat or belittle, you preserve the dignity and self-respect of both parties, paving the way for more amicable interactions in the future. Divorce is already a difficult process, and adding insult to injury only extends the pain.

Day 163

Even though it's difficult, treat each other with as much respect as you would a stranger.

While the marriage no longer remains intact, the basic human dignity and decency owed to one another does. Just as you strive to show kindness and courtesy to strangers, extending the same courtesy to your ex-partner can help foster an environment of civility and mutual understanding, diffuse conflicts, reduce animosity, and pave the way for constructive communication. It may require effort and patience, but by upholding a standard of respect, you not only honor the inherent worth of our ex-partner but also preserve your own integrity and self-respect.

Day 164

Fear and doubt are usually due to a lack of communication.

During divorce, the absence of clear communication can exacerbate the already painful process, intensifying confusion, resentment, and isolation. When divorcing couples cannot communicate effectively, they often find themselves embroiled in bitter disputes fueled by misunderstandings and unexpressed grievances. Without open dialogue, unresolved issues linger, festering beneath the surface and hindering progress toward amicable resolutions. The lack of communication can perpetuate feelings of loneliness and abandonment, as each partner struggles to make sense of the situation without the support and understanding of the other. By recognizing the importance of communication and attempting to engage in constructive dialogue, divorcing couples can navigate the process with greater empathy and cooperation. Through therapy, mediation, or simply a willingness to listen, you can unravel the complexities of the relationship, find closure, and embark on separate paths with newfound clarity and understanding.

Day 165

The less you respond to negative people, the more peaceful your life will become.

By refusing to be drawn into arguments or confrontations, you keep your inner peace and emotional well-being. This doesn't mean ignoring important issues or failing to stand up for yourself when needed, but rather, it involves prioritizing your mental and emotional health by not allowing negativity to take root. This doesn't just go for your soon-to-be ex-spouse. Use this tactic for anyone you encounter.

Day 166

You can choose how you respond to even the most difficult situations. Stand strong in the face of chaos.

Empower yourself to not just survive, but to thrive despite the challenges you may encounter. By maintaining this mindset, you take charge of your well-being and resilience. Instead of letting difficult situations dictate your emotions, focus on finding strength within yourself to overcome them. Embrace the opportunity for growth and transformation, using each obstacle as a stepping stone to a brighter future. Remember, your response to adversity can shape your journey through divorce and beyond. Choose to respond with courage, determination, and positivity, and you'll emerge stronger and more resilient than ever before.

Day 167

Before you say anything, ask yourself,
"Is it true? Is it kind? Is it necessary?"

Before uttering a single word, stop and ask yourself a series of critical questions: is what I'm about to say true? Is it kind? Is it necessary? This serves as a powerful filter, guiding you toward responses that are both constructive and compassionate. This mindful approach to dialogue cultivates an environment of respect and empathy, laying the groundwork for constructive co-parenting and future relationships.

Day 168

Before responding to your ex-spouse's attempt to
communicate, ask yourself if it really needs a response.

Not every communication requires a response, especially if it pertains to trivial comments that have the potential to escalate into unnecessary conflicts. By adopting a selective approach to responding, you can mitigate the risk of being drawn into contentious exchanges that serve no constructive purpose. Instead, prioritize addressing issues that are pertinent to the well-being of both parties involved, particularly matters concerning children or financial arrangements. The goal is to keep a level of detachment from petty disputes and focus on facilitating a smoother transition into separate lives.

Day 169

*Knee-jerk response can lead to further
misunderstandings or conflict.*

During divorce proceedings, emotions can run high, and the temptation to react impulsively to communication may be strong. Take a moment to pause and consider the implications of your response. Reflect on whether your words align with your long-term goals and the relationship you wish to cultivate post-divorce. By choosing your words carefully and approaching interactions with mindfulness, you can minimize the risk of conflict and work to resolve disputes constructively.

Day 170

Create and respect new boundaries.

Establishing boundaries will define personal space, emotional limits, and acceptable behavior for both parties. Respect for these boundaries is crucial to keeping a healthy post-divorce relationship, especially when co-parenting or sharing assets. It's important to recognize and acknowledge these new boundaries, even if they may feel uncomfortable or restrictive at first. By respecting each other's space and boundaries, former spouses can create a more amicable and cooperative environment and help both of you focus on your own healing and personal growth, rather than getting entangled in unnecessary conflicts or power struggles.

Day 171

Communicate only what is necessary.

When interacting with your soon-to-be ex-spouse, it's crucial to communicate only what is necessary or relevant to the matter at hand. By focusing on essential matters, such as legal arrangements, co-parenting responsibilities, and financial agreements, both parties can maintain clarity and efficiency throughout the divorce process. It also reduces the likelihood of emotional conflicts or unnecessary confrontations, allowing both parties to navigate the divorce proceedings with greater ease and cooperation.

Day 172

Don't belittle your former spouse or instigate conflict.

During a divorce, it's crucial to not belittle your former spouse or instigate conflict with them. Engaging in such behavior not only reflects poorly on your character, but can also escalate tensions and prolong the divorce process. Instead, strive to maintain a level of civility and respect, even in difficult circumstances. By choosing to take the high road and avoid derogatory remarks or antagonistic behavior, you show maturity and integrity, which can facilitate smoother negotiations and a more amicable resolution.

Day 173

Don't track your former spouse's location or record conversations without permission.

Monitoring or recording your soon-to-be ex-spouse without their consent is not only a breach of privacy, but also a violation of trust that can significantly escalate tensions during divorce proceedings. Such actions not only show a lack of respect for boundaries, but also creates an atmosphere of distrust and hostility, further complicating an already challenging situation. Besides being unethical, tracking or recording conversations without permission may also have legal implications depending on the jurisdiction, potentially leading to legal consequences for the individual responsible. You can, however, keep a written account of interactions for your own record and reference.

Day 174

Don't rehash the reasons for getting a divorce.

While it's natural to want closure or validation for the decision to end the marriage, dwelling on past grievances only delays the healing process. Rehashing the reasons for divorce often devolves into blame shifting and arguments, creating a toxic cycle of conflict that hinders any chance of amicable resolution. Instead, focus on accepting the reality of the situation and directing your energy toward constructive endeavors.

Chapter 6
*Child-Centered Choices:
Prioritizing Kids Every
Step of the Way*

Day 175

*Beforehand, have a discussion together about how you
will tell your children and how you and your soon-to-be
former spouse will explain the separation. Don't
assume your partner won't cooperate.*

In breaking the news of divorce to your children, teamwork and communication are key. Sit with your soon-to-be ex-spouse beforehand and discuss how you'll approach this delicate conversation. It's crucial not to make assumptions about your partner's willingness to cooperate—open and honest communication is essential. By planning together, you can ensure that you and your ex-partner deliver the message in a unified and supportive manner, which can help ease some of the confusion and anxiety your children may experience.

Day 176

Love your children more than you dislike your ex.

Regardless of any animosity or discord between you and your ex-partner, ensure that your love and devotion to your children stays unwavering. Resist the temptation to allow negative feelings or resentments toward your ex to overshadow your parental responsibilities. Focus efforts on fostering a supportive and nurturing environment for your children where they feel valued, cherished, and emotionally secure.

Day 177

Reassure your children that both parents love them.

Take the time to communicate openly and often with your children, emphasizing that while the family dynamic may be changing, your love for them is not. Encourage them to express their feelings and concerns and validate their emotions. Remind them they are not to blame for the divorce and that both you and your ex-spouse are committed to supporting them through this transition. This advice goes for children of all ages. By consistently reaffirming your love and support, you can help address any feelings of insecurity or abandonment your children may experience during this challenging time.

Day 178

Be careful not to use your children as a therapist.
You'll screw them up more than help yourself.

Divorce will be emotionally taxing for both parents and children, often leaving each person in need of an outlet for feelings and frustrations. However, relying on children as therapy can have detrimental effects on their emotional well-being. While it may seem natural to confide in children, sharing adult concerns or burdens with them can overwhelm them and blur the boundaries between parent and child roles. Children may feel burdened by the weight of their parents' problems, causing them undue stress and anxiety. Using your child as a therapist can also hinder children's ability to focus on their own development and growth, impeding their emotional resilience and coping mechanisms. Instead of burdening children with adult issues, parents should seek support from friends, family members, or professional therapists to provide proper guidance and help.

Day 179

When your children want to talk and share their problems, stop everything and listen without judgment.

Children of divorce often grapple with complex emotions and uncertainties, seeking reassurance and understanding from their parents. By prioritizing open communication and active listening, parents can create a safe and supportive environment where children feel valued and heard. Children can often be reluctant to share their feelings, but when they are ready to talk, it's important to set aside distractions and agendas to prioritize meaningful interactions with them, strengthening trust and emotional connection. By offering unconditional support and empathy, parents can help children navigate the challenges of divorce with resilience and confidence, empowering them to express their feelings and seek guidance without fear of judgment or dismissal.

Day 180

Children may feel as though they are the cause of the divorce. Do all you can to assure them this is not the case.

Children often internalize the upheaval of divorce, mistakenly believing that they are to blame for the dissolution of their parents' marriage. It's essential to take proactive steps to reassure them that this is not the case. Start open and honest conversations with your children, emphasizing that the decision to divorce is between adults and not a reflection of their worth or actions. Validate their feelings of confusion and sadness, while gently correcting any misconceptions they may have about their role in the situation. Encourage them to express their emotions freely and provide consistent reassurance that both parents love them unconditionally.

Day 181

Children need a safe space to share their emotions.

As a parent, you play a pivotal role in creating this space, but it's also essential to enlist the support of trusted adults who can offer additional guidance and support. Whether it's a close family member, a trusted teacher, or a compassionate counselor, identify individuals whom your children feel comfortable confiding in and encourage them to reach out for unbiased support when needed.

Day 182

Don't badmouth your spouse in front of your children.

Don't badmouth your spouse in front of your kids, as negative comments can inflict lasting harm on their emotional and psychological health. Instead, strive to maintain a respectful and amicable demeanor, both in your interactions with your ex-partner and in the presence of your children. Foster open lines of communication with your kids, encouraging them to express their feelings and concerns without fear of judgment or reprisal. Even though your feelings for your former spouse have changed, it's important for your children to feel love from both of you.

Day 183

When you talk badly about the child's other parent, the child does not think better of you or worse of the other parent; they think worse of themselves.

When you negatively talk about a child's other parent, the repercussions extend far beyond your intended target. It's crucial to realize that children absorb these conversations differently than adults do. Rather than forming negative opinions about the other parent, children often internalize these remarks, leading them to question their own worth and identity. Instead of enhancing your image in their eyes, you inadvertently tarnish their sense of self-worth and belonging.

Day 184

Do not hold your children as leverage in negotiations.

By separating parenting responsibilities from financial matters, you can maintain a supportive and cooperative co-parenting relationship, fostering a stable and nurturing environment for your children during and after the divorce process. Ultimately, safeguarding your children's emotional well-being and protecting them from the stress of financial negotiations is a priority, laying the foundation for a healthy and harmonious co-parenting dynamic in the years to come.

Day 185

Learn to separate your feelings for your former spouse from their ability to be a good parent.

Despite any conflicts or differences between you and your ex-partner, acknowledging their ability to be a good parent is essential for the well-being of your children. While they may differ from yours, recognizing and appreciating their positive attributes as a parent, even if they were not the best partner, can contribute to fostering a healthy co-parenting dynamic. By prioritizing the best interests of your children and supporting a cooperative relationship with your former spouse, you create an environment where your children can benefit from having two loving and involved parents in their lives.

Day 186

Spouses divorce. Parents are forever.

It's crucial to recognize that while spouses may part ways, their responsibilities and commitments as parents endure indefinitely. Even amidst the challenges and complexities of divorce, prioritizing the well-being and best interests of the children is important. Above all else, both parents must strive to keep open lines of communication, foster a positive co-parenting dynamic, and prioritize their children's emotional and psychological needs.

Day 187

Recognize and respect the wide range of emotions your children have about the divorce.

From confusion and sadness to anger and frustration, each child may respond differently to the upheaval of their family dynamic. By recognizing and confirming these emotions, you create a safe and supportive environment where your children feel heard and understood. It's critical to encourage open communication channels so your children can openly express their feelings without fear of judgment. Through empathetic listening and unwavering support, you can help your children navigate the complexities of divorce with resilience and grace.

Day 188

The decisions you'll make during the divorce process will affect you and your children for years to come.

Focus on prioritizing the well-being and best interests of all parties involved, especially your children. Rather than fixating on semantics or winning arguments, direct your energy toward finding fair solutions that promote stability and harmony. Stay focused on the goal of navigating the divorce process with dignity and respect, laying the groundwork for a positive and cooperative co-parenting relationship in the years to come.

Day 189

Don't depend on children to fill your emotional needs.

While parental love and support are essential for children's well-being, expecting kids to fulfill all emotional needs places undue pressure on them and can delay their own growth and development. Instead, you must cultivate fulfilling relationships, hobbies, and activities outside of your role as parents to fulfill your emotional needs. This not only fosters independence and resilience within individuals, but also creates a more balanced and harmonious family dynamic. By nurturing your emotional well-being independently, you can model healthy behaviors for your children and create a supportive environment where everyone acknowledges and respects each other's needs.

Day 190

If a child's struggles continue, it usually has something to do with the differences in environments or discipline between the two homes.

When children show prolonged distress during divorce, it's essential to consider various factors that may contribute to their emotional struggles. Ineffective discipline methods, such as inconsistent boundaries or overly harsh punishments or overly lenient parenting styles, can leave children feeling confused and insecure. Insufficient displays of affection and emotional support from parents may worsen feelings of abandonment and isolation in children, intensifying their distress. Placing excessive emotional or practical responsibilities on children, such as confiding in them about adult issues or expecting them to take on caregiving roles, can overwhelm them and hinder their ability to cope effectively. As parents navigate divorce, it's crucial to prioritize their children's emotional well-being by providing consistent discipline, ample affection, and age-appropriate responsibilities.

Day 191

Treat your children as children—not as adults.

While it may be tempting to confide in your children or seek solace in their presence, it's important to maintain boundaries and protect their innocence. Do not involve them in discussions about finances or custody arrangements, as this information can overwhelm and confuse them. Instead, prioritize their emotional well-being by providing them with love, stability, and reassurance.

Day 192

Before talking to the kids about divorce, get a few age-appropriate books that speak to them about divorce.

Age-appropriate books about divorce offer valuable insight, helping children feel less alone and more supported. By introducing these books into your discussions, you can create a safe and nurturing environment where your children feel empowered to express their emotions and ask questions. It's good practice to read the books for yourself before giving them to your children, so you have a point of reference should they want to talk about what they read. Reading together can also strengthen the parent-child bond and encourage open communication channels, laying the foundation for ongoing dialogue and support throughout the divorce process.

Day 193

Your child will be on an emotional rollercoaster too.

Like adults, kids experience a rollercoaster of emotions throughout the divorce process. Parents need to recognize and validate these feelings, creating a supportive environment where children feel safe expressing themselves. Encouraging open communication and providing reassurance can comfort children and remind them that their feelings are normal and that they are not alone in their experiences.

Day 194

When it comes to children, consistency in schedules and rules makes life less stressful for everyone.

Maintaining stable routines across households helps ease stress and uncertainty for both parents and children. Consistent schedules for activities, such as mealtimes, bedtime, and school routines provide a sense of predictability and security for children, helping establish emotional stability during a time of upheaval. Enforcing consistent rules and expectations across households promotes fairness and reduces confusion for children. When children know what to expect and understand the boundaries in place, they feel more secure and are better equipped to cope with the changes brought about by divorce

Day 195

Discuss visitation arrangements with your former spouse before sharing with your children.

Before discussing visitation arrangements with your children, it's crucial to have a thoughtful and constructive conversation with your spouse. This approach allows for the consideration of several factors, such as the children's school schedules, extracurricular activities, and individual preferences. Presenting a united front to the children is another way parents can provide reassurance and stability during the transition period.

Day 196

Do not use your child as a communication link to your former spouse.

Don't even think about it! Using your children as a messenger between you and your ex-spouse places undue stress and an emotional burden on them. While it might seem convenient or less confrontational in the short-term, it can have long-lasting negative effects on your child's well-being and relationship with both parents. Instead, prioritize open, direct communication with your ex-partner, whether it's through face-to-face conversations, phone calls, or emails.

Day 197

Do not embellish or make up stories about the other parent, so you get more time with the children.

Fabricating stories or exaggerating the truth about the other parent to gain favor or secure more time with the children is harmful and unfair. It not only damages the children's trust in both parents but also creates confusion and emotional distress. Children deserve to have authentic relationships with both parents, free from manipulation and deceit. Instead of resorting to dishonest tactics, prioritize honesty and transparency in your interactions with your children. Encourage open communication and reassure them that both parents love and care for them deeply, regardless of any differences between you and your ex-partner.

Day 198

As you begin co-parenting, recognize you both will do things differently.

Rather than viewing differences in parenting styles as right or wrong, approach them with understanding and flexibility. Embracing an open-minded mindset paves the way for cooperation and harmony, enhancing the well-being of your children. Emphasizing mutual respect and communication allows both parents to contribute positively to their children's upbringing.

Day 199

The more positive you are during the transition and handoff to the other parent, the more comfortable the process will be for the children.

Maintaining a positive attitude during these transitions can help ease their anxieties and uncertainties. By projecting calmness and reassurance, you show your children that despite the changes, they can still feel secure in their relationships with both parents. Ideally, children should feel content with both parents, even during transitions between homes. It's essential to avoid introducing new topics or nitpicking over minor issues during hand-offs. Instead, prioritize creating an upbeat atmosphere for the children's sake.

Day 200

Children need a sense of stability.

Even if they don't express it verbally, they have concerns about where they will live, when they will see each parent, where they'll keep their belongings, and whether both parents still love them. Parents must address these unspoken worries by providing clear and consistent information about the practical aspects of their new living arrangements. Parents should prioritize creating a sense of stability by keeping routines, providing emotional support, and reassuring their children of their unconditional love and commitment to their well-being.

Day 201

There is no universally perfect type of legal or physical custody arrangement. You must work together to determine what is right for your children.

When navigating divorce, it's essential to recognize that there is no one-size-fits-all solution when it comes to legal or physical custody arrangements. Each family's circumstances and dynamics are unique, requiring careful consideration and collaboration between parents to figure out what is in the best interest of their children. This often involves open communication, compromise, and flexibility to create arrangements that create positive relationships between children and both parents. By working together and prioritizing the children's needs, parents can develop custody arrangements that promote stability, security, and healthy development for their children as they adjust to the changes in their family structure.

Day 202

Each household needs clear and reasonable rules about bedtime, responsibilities, and proper behavior.

Consistency between households helps children understand what you expect of them and reduces confusion and stress. Parents need to communicate and collaborate on setting these rules, ensuring that they align with the family's values and priorities. By setting up a consistent framework of rules and expectations, parents can create a sense of security and predictability for their children, which is especially important during times of transition. Just like you two might not have agreed on everything before, you can bet there'll be differences in how you both parent after the split. The key? Consistency. Try to keep things as steady as you can between both households, but realize there's bound to be some variations. Instead of locking horns over those differences, aim for a compromise, find that middle ground, and then keep moving forward.

Day 203

Parents often have a hard time being objective in evaluating how their children are coping. Input from teachers or daycare providers can be invaluable.

It's common for parents to struggle with objectivity when assessing how their children are coping with divorce. Seeking input from teachers or daycare providers can provide a valuable perspective on a child's behavior and emotional well-being outside of the home environment. These professionals interact with children in various settings and may notice changes or patterns that parents might overlook. They can offer insight into a child's social interactions, academic performance, and overall adjustment, helping parents gain a more comprehensive understanding of their child's experience. By collaborating with educators and caregivers, parents can access added support and resources to address any concerns and ensure that their children receive support during this challenging time.

Day 204

*If children have ongoing struggles, it may be tied
to ongoing parental dynamics.*

Children may struggle with feelings of instability, confusion, and insecurity if family relationships are still tense or contentious post-divorce. Addressing these ongoing challenges is crucial for supporting children's emotional well-being and helping them navigate the transition more effectively. Know that the resolution to a child's continued struggles may lie with the dynamics of their parents just as much as within themselves.

Day 206

*As part of respecting your child's emotions, do
your best to just listen and not intervene.*

When your child expresses their feelings, whether it's sadness, anger, or confusion, the best thing to do is create a safe space for them to share openly. Avoid the urge to minimize their emotions or offer quick solutions. Instead, confirm their feelings by acknowledging them and providing empathy and support. Practice active listening by giving your full attention, keeping eye contact, and showing understanding through verbal and nonverbal cues. Resist the temptation to jump in with advice or explanations; sometimes, all your child needs is to be heard and understood.

Day 205

Let your children express their emotions, but don't mistakenly send the message that you will be sad if your child is sad. Let their feelings be theirs.

During divorce, it's crucial to create an environment where children feel comfortable expressing their emotions without feeling responsible for their parent's feelings. While it's natural for parents to empathize with their children's sadness or anger, it's essential to avoid conveying that their emotions directly affect your well-being. Encourage your children to express themselves openly and validate their feelings without attaching your emotional state to theirs. Let them know that it's okay to feel sad, angry, or confused, and reassure them you're there to support them through these emotions. Your role as a parent is to provide a safe space for them to navigate their emotions while offering unconditional love and support, regardless of your own emotional state.

Day 207

If your child shows signs of ongoing anxiety, it could be from a lack of structure or consistency.

Children experiencing ongoing anxiety during divorce may benefit from clear structures and routines to provide stability and predictability in their lives. One simple idea is to post a schedule prominently where they can easily see it, which will offer them reassurance and a sense of control. The schedule serves as a reference point, helping them understand what to expect and when. Consistent routines, such as set mealtimes, bedtime rituals, and designated homework hours, can create a comforting sense of order and familiarity, which could help ease stress. If your child has extracurricular activities, post these to the schedule along with how they are getting to and from the activity, such as if Mom is taking them to soccer and the other parent is bringing them home. Having your children create the schedule empowers them and fosters a sense of ownership over their routines, which leads to feelings of security and stability.

Day 208

Be available to talk without judgment when your children are ready.

Giving children the freedom to retreat into their own thoughts and feelings allows them to process their emotions at their own pace, fostering a sense of autonomy and control during a tumultuous time. However, it's equally important for parents to maintain open lines of communication and reassure their children that they are always available to listen without judgment whenever they feel ready to share.

Day 209

Without structure, children may test boundaries and misbehave to gain attention.

Consistency in routines and expectations, especially across both households, can minimize these issues by providing children with a sense of predictability and security amidst the changes. When parents keep similar structures for bedtime, meals, chores, and homework, children are less likely to feel unsettled by the transition between homes. They will know what both parents expect of them and may be less likely to try to get away with misbehaving.

Day 210

Alert teachers and other caregivers that your family is going through a divorce, so your child can receive extra support as needed.

By informing teachers and other caregivers about the divorce, you enable them to offer extra support to your child. They often see a different side of the child than parents see at home. It also fosters a collaborative relationship between parents and caregivers, allowing them to work together in the best interest of the child's emotional and academic success despite the family's challenges.

Day 211

Be a model of calmness.

Children are incredibly perceptive and can pick up on tension and discord within the family environment, which can be emotionally distressing. Being a model of composure amidst the challenges of divorce can provide children with a sense of stability and security. By showing resilience and handling disagreements or conflicts with grace, you can instill valuable coping skills in your children. Insulating children from the brunt of parental conflicts helps preserve their emotional well-being, fosters their emotional resilience, and promotes their overall adjustment to the changes occurring within the family.

Day 212

If your former spouse is not cooperative, do your best to set routines and expectations for your home, since you have control over that.

Establishing routines and expectations within your household can provide stability and predictability for your children amidst the changes brought on by divorce. By setting clear guidelines, schedules, and boundaries, you create a sense of security and structure for your children, helping them feel more grounded.

Day 213

The intensity of conflict between parents hurts children more than the divorce itself.

While divorce introduces changes and challenges in children's lives, it is often conflict and hostility between parents that inflicts the most significant emotional wounds. High levels of conflict can create an environment of stress, anxiety, and instability for children, leading to long-lasting emotional and psychological repercussions. It is important to minimize conflict and prioritize effective communication and cooperation for the sake of their children's emotional health and development.

Day 214

Be supportive of the time your child spends with the other parent. Let them know it's okay to be happy when they're with the other parent.

It's essential to recognize that both parents play vital roles in a child's life, regardless of the relationship status between the parents. Encouraging and facilitating a positive relationship between your child and their other parent shows respect for their bond and helps foster a sense of security and stability for the child. By encouraging regular and meaningful contact with the other parent, you promote a sense of belonging and connection for your child, which is essential for their overall emotional health. Supporting the relationship with the other parent can also help ease any feelings of guilt or loyalty conflicts that your child may experience, allowing them to keep healthy and loving relationships with both parents despite the divorce.

Day 215

Maintaining routines gives your child a sense of peace and stability when other areas of their life are changing.

Maintaining routines provides children with a much-needed sense of stability and security. Routines offer predictability and familiarity in a time of upheaval, helping children navigate the transition with a greater sense of peace and comfort. Consistent routines, such as regular mealtimes, bedtime rituals, and extracurricular activities, create a reliable structure that children can rely on amidst the changes occurring in their family life. By adhering to routines, parents can reassure their children that despite the divorce, some aspects of their lives are still constant and dependable. This stability helps ease feelings of uncertainty and anxiety, promoting emotional well-being and resilience in children as they adjust to new circumstances. Keeping routines can also ease a smoother transition between households in shared custody arrangements, providing a sense of continuity and normalcy for children as they move between different environments.

Day 216

When you begin dating again, insulate your children from the new person until you are sure the relationship is strong and healthy. Even then, do not force your children to have a relationship with the new person.

Following a divorce, children often need time to adjust to the changes in their family dynamic and may experience feelings of confusion, insecurity, or loyalty conflicts. Parents must prioritize their children's emotional well-being by refraining from introducing them to new romantic partners until the relationship is stable and likely to endure. Rushing into introductions prematurely can create unnecessary stress and anxiety for children, potentially causing further disruption to their sense of security and stability. By shielding children from new relationships until the timing is right and ensuring that the relationship is strong and healthy, parents can mitigate potential negative impact and foster a supportive environment for their children's emotional growth and development.

PS: Recognize that you may be head over heels happy for the new relationship, but it may take considerable time for your children to accept the new dynamic. You cannot and should not force your children to accept the new person.

Day 217

Co-parenting is not a competition, but a collaboration of parents doing what is best for the kids.

Instead of viewing co-parenting as a competition or battleground, co-parenting should be seen as a joint venture aimed at providing a stable, nurturing, and supportive environment for children to thrive. Effective co-parenting involves open communication, mutual respect, and a willingness to compromise for the sake of the children. By putting aside personal differences and focusing on the common goal of raising happy and healthy children, parents can create a positive co-parenting dynamic that minimizes the negative impact of divorce on children.

Day 218

Children should not have to sacrifice so that you can have the life you want. Parents must make sacrifices so their children can have the life they deserve.

Rather than expecting children to sacrifice their well-being or happiness for the sake of their parents' desires or lifestyle choices, parents should make sacrifices themselves to provide their children with the love, support, and stability they deserve.

Day 219

*Kids are sensitive to rejection, criticism, and anger.
They deserve to grow up in place where they feel
safe, accepted, and loved.*

Divorce often introduces heightened levels of stress, conflict, and instability into children's lives, making them particularly susceptible to negative experiences, such as rejection, ridicule, criticism, and anger within the home. However, children deserve to grow up in an environment characterized by safety, acceptance, and warmth, where they feel valued, supported, and loved unconditionally. Amidst the challenges of divorce, parents need to prioritize creating a nurturing and supportive environment for their children, one that promotes emotional security, fosters positive self-esteem, and encourages healthy development. By providing a safe and loving home environment, parents can mitigate the negative effects of divorce on children and help them navigate the complexities of family separation with resilience and strength.

Day 220

Instead of raising kids who turn out okay despite their childhood, let's raise kids who turn out amazing because of their childhood.

Divorce often introduces challenges and disruptions in children's lives, potentially affecting their emotional and psychological development. However, rather than viewing divorce solely as a hindrance to children's well-being, this quote encourages parents to transform adversity into opportunity by fostering an environment conducive to growth, resilience, and personal development. By prioritizing love, support, and positive reinforcement, parents can empower their children to navigate the challenges of divorce with strength, ultimately emerging as extraordinary individuals shaped by their experiences. This perspective highlights the transformative power of parental guidance and support in shaping children's futures, emphasizing the potential for growth and success even in the face of adversity.

Day 221

When you truly listen to your child, they grow up believing they have a voice that matters.

When your child speaks, give them your full attention: make eye contact, nod in understanding, and ask questions to show you are engaged. Avoid interrupting or dismissing their feelings, even if they express anger, sadness, or confusion. Let them know their thoughts and feelings matter and that it is safe to share them with you. This approach teaches your child the importance of open communication and respect. By being a reliable and empathetic listener, you empower your child to develop their own voice and confidence.

Day 222

Children are always watching and listening!

Showing your children that divorcing parents can respect each other will give them a good foundation for the conflict that arises in their own lives. When engaging with your former spouse, do your best to remain relaxed and focused. Use a calm tone and a concerned facial expression when tensions arise. If a conversation is getting away from you, it's okay to say that you need a break to calm down, and then return to finish when you're in a better state of mind. This shows your child that not every conversation will be smooth or resolved quickly and that it's important to remain respectful.

Day 223

*The best interest of the child isn't alienating
them from a loving parent or stepparent.*

The best interests of children lie in maintaining positive and supportive connections with all caring individuals in their lives, including both biological and through marriage. Children benefit from having strong and nurturing relationships with all parental figures, as these relationships contribute to their emotional security, sense of belonging, and overall well-being.

Day 224

*When parents respect each other, children
have a greater sense of security.*

Divorce will introduce uncertainties in children's lives, leading to feelings of insecurity and anxiety. However, when parents prove mutual respect and civility toward each other, it creates a sense of stability, reassurance, and security for their children. Children thrive in environments where they feel safe, loved, and supported, and parental respect serves as a crucial foundation for building trust and emotional security amidst the challenges of family separation. By modeling respectful communication and cooperation, you can help minimize the negative effects of divorce on your children.

Day 225

Children are not possessions. You do not 'allow' a parent extra time. When you say things like that, you imply you think of your children as things, not humans.

Divorce can sometimes lead to disputes over custody and visitation rights, with children being unintentionally viewed as objects or assets to be divided. However, this quote emphasizes that children are people too, with emotions and needs that you must respect and prioritize above parental disputes. They deserve to be treated with dignity, love, and care, regardless of the circumstances surrounding their parents' separation.

Day 226

Children will always remember who showed up, not who texted once or twice a year.

While cell phones and email can make communication easy, children often value and remember the tangible presence and support of their parents. Divorce will introduce uncertainty in children's lives, leading them to seek stability, reassurance, and emotional support from both parents. It is important to prioritize quality time and meaningful interactions with your children, despite the challenges of divorce. By proving their commitment, dedication, and love through physical presence and active participation in your children's lives, you will foster strong bonds, trust, and emotional connection.

Day 227

The intensity of conflict between parents hurts children more than the divorce itself.

While divorce introduces changes and challenges in children's lives, it is often conflict and hostility between parents that inflicts the most significant emotional wounds. High levels of conflict can create an environment of stress, anxiety, and instability for children, leading to long-lasting emotional and psychological repercussions. It is important to minimize conflict and prioritize effective communication and cooperation for the sake of their children's emotional health and development.

Day 228

Children care about who takes them to practice and cheers them on from the stands.

Do not take for granted or minimize the significance of providing encouragement from the sidelines, whether it be attending sports practices, music lessons, or other activities. Your children will look from the stage or playing field to find their parents in the crowd. They will beam with happiness to see you cheering them on. By taking an active role in your children's lives and showing support and enthusiasm for their interests and passions, you are developing a sense of security, belonging, and emotional connection for them.

Day 229

The hurt you cause your children will often stay and develop with them, defining who they become.

The hurt inflicted on children during this tumultuous time can linger, influencing their perceptions of themselves, relationships, and the world around them. When parents cannot navigate divorce with sensitivity and consideration for their children's well-being, the resulting emotional trauma can become deeply ingrained, affecting their self-esteem, trust in others, and ability to form healthy connections. The wounds inflicted by parental animosity can manifest in various ways, from struggles with intimacy and communication to difficulty regulating emotions and coping with stress. As children grow, these unresolved issues may continue to manifest, affecting their choices, behaviors, and overall quality of life. Therefore, parents must prioritize their children's emotional needs during divorce, fostering an environment of love, support, and stability to mitigate the long-term consequences of their actions. By providing reassurance, understanding, and guidance, parents can help their children emerge as resilient individuals, capable of building fulfilling lives despite the pain of their past.

Day 230

Children care about who is in the audience during their first recital.

Divorce can bring about changes in family dynamics and routines, leading children to seek reassurance and validation from their parents amidst the uncertainties. This bit of wisdom highlights the importance of parents prioritizing their children's emotional well-being and actively taking part in significant moments, such as recitals, performances, and achievements. By being present in the audience and showing their support, parents prove their love, encouragement, and pride in their children's accomplishments, regardless of the challenges or obstacles they may be personally facing. It emphasizes the value of parental involvement, engagement, and emotional connection in fostering children's confidence, self-esteem, and sense of belonging amidst the complexities of divorce.

Day 231

The goal of every parent should be to raise children who do not have to recover from their childhood.

Your goal as a parent should be to nurture your children in a way where they don't have to spend their adult lives trying to heal from their past. Instead of creating wounds that need healing later, focus on fostering an environment of love, support, and understanding. By prioritizing your children's emotional well-being and providing them with the tools to navigate life's challenges, we set them on a path toward a fulfilling and balanced adulthood. It's not about shielding them from every hardship, but equipping them with the resilience.

Day 232

A child cannot have too many people who love them and want them to succeed.

Especially during divorce, children need to feel surrounded by a network of caring and supportive individuals who are invested in their well-being and success. Of course, family is important, but there is a significance in extended family members, friends, mentors, and any other trusted individual who plays a role in providing emotional support, guidance, and encouragement to children during the divorce process. Your children's cheering section can never be too large!

131

Day 233

A real parent is someone who puts that child above their own selfish needs and wants.

A real parent recognizes that their children's needs must always come first, even during personal struggles or disagreements with their co-parent. There is an emphasis on the selflessness of a parent and the unconditional love needed from parents to prioritize their children's emotional security, stability, and happiness over their own desires for convenience or comfort.

Day 234

Be the parent your inner child never had.

Divorce can evoke deep-seated emotions and unresolved issues from one's own upbringing, which may manifest in parenting practices and interactions with their children. By acknowledging and addressing these inner child wounds, parents can cultivate greater empathy, understanding, and emotional connection with their children during the divorce process. It is important to break generational cycles of neglect or dysfunction by consciously embodying the qualities of compassionate and supportive caregiving that may have been absent in one's own upbringing.

Day 235

Children care about who stayed until two o'clock in the morning to finish their costume for the school play.

Divorce can bring about changes in family dynamics and routines, leading children to seek reassurance and support from their parents amidst the uncertainties. Parents need to prove their commitment and presence in their children's lives, regardless of the challenges or obstacles they may face. By prioritizing quality time, active participation, and emotional support, parents can foster strong bonds with their children and create lasting memories that outweigh the complexities of divorce. There is value in parental dedication, effort, and sacrifice when nurturing children's emotional well-being and helping them navigate the transitions and uncertainties associated with family separation. Ultimately, children cherish the moments when their parents are actively involved and present in their lives, regardless of the circumstances.

Day 236

The tragedy of staying in an unhappy marriage is teaching your children the wrong things about love.

Staying in a toxic or unfulfilling marriage not only perpetuates a cycle of dysfunction, but also models unhealthy relationship dynamics for children. By seeing conflict, resentment, or emotional neglect between parents, children may internalize skewed beliefs of love and intimacy, potentially influencing their own future relationships. In contrast, divorce, when approached with empathy and honesty, can catalyze growth and authenticity. It teaches children the importance of self-respect, boundaries, and prioritizing emotional health in relationships.

Day 237

Children become spoiled when we substitute gifts for time.

While material gifts may momentarily distract from the upheaval, they cannot replace the enduring impact of parental involvement and emotional availability. In divorce, maintaining a strong presence in children's lives through consistent communication, quality time, and emotional support becomes paramount.

Day 238

*If you spread rumors, you will only end up
hurting your kids and looking petty.*

While it may be tempting to vent frustrations or seek validation from others by sharing stories or rumors, doing so can have detrimental effects, particularly on your children and your reputation. Children are highly perceptive and can be deeply affected by negative comments or rumors about one of their parents, leading to confusion, insecurity, and emotional distress. Spreading rumors also reflects poorly on your character, potentially undermining your credibility and integrity in the eyes of others.

Day 239

*If you have children, all hand-offs should
take place in a safe location.*

Ensuring the safety and well-being of children during and after divorce is vital, and this includes setting up safe locations for transitions between parents. Safe locations provide a neutral and secure environment where children can move between parental homes without feeling anxious or exposed to potential conflict. The location can even be a happy place for the child, like a favorite park.

Day 240

*When working through custody and child support,
take expectations for college savings
for each child into consideration.*

It's important to consider the long-term financial implications for your children, including their educational future. Discussing and agreeing upon how to manage future college expenses can help ease potential conflicts down the road and ensure that both parents are financially prepared to help support their children's higher education aspirations. This may involve setting up a plan for contributing to college savings accounts, such as 529 plans, or agreeing on if and how you will divide college expenses. Receipt of the first tuition bill is not the time to learn your former spouse had no intention of helping pay for the child's college education. By proactively addressing college savings during divorce proceedings, you can create a clear financial roadmap for your children's educational goals and provide them with the support they need to pursue higher education without added stress or financial strain.

Day 241

Give the other parent the first right of
refusal when caring for the kids.

By allowing your former spouse to spend added time with the children when you cannot care for them, you show a willingness to prioritize the children's well-being and support a cooperative co-parenting relationship. This gesture fosters trust and mutual respect between both parties, as it shows a commitment to working together in the best interests of the children despite the challenges of the divorce process. Providing the first right of refusal can also prevent potential conflicts over childcare arrangements and scheduling disagreements, as both parents have clear expectations and opportunities to take part in their children's lives. Overall, this approach promotes a healthier co-parenting environment and helps ensure that the children's needs stay a top priority throughout the divorce proceedings and beyond.

Day 242

Don't supervise your children's
communication with the other parent.

Respecting your children's autonomy and fostering open communication with the other parent is crucial in mitigating the impact of divorce on their well-being. Hovering over their interactions with the other parent can create feelings of anxiety, confusion, and resentment, undermining their sense of trust and security. By allowing your children the freedom to communicate freely with the other parent, you empower them to maintain healthy relationships and navigate the complexities of divorce with greater comfort. Supervising their interactions may send the message that you don't trust their judgment or are trying to undermine their bond with the other parent, further exacerbating the emotional toll of divorce. Instead, encourage open dialogue, listen to their concerns, and support their efforts to maintain meaningful connections with both you and their other parent.

Chapter 7
*Boundaries and Balance:
The Importance of Self-care*

Day 243

*Sometimes, you just have to laugh instead of cry or
cry yourself into a laughing fit. Both are okay.*

Laughter has the remarkable ability to lighten the emotional burden and brings a sense of levity to even the darkest moments. On the other hand, crying can serve as a cathartic release, allowing you to express and process your emotions healthily and authentically. There may be times when laughter and tears intertwine, blurring the lines between joy and sorrow. In these moments, allow yourself to surrender to the full spectrum of your emotions, embracing the complexity of your experience without judgment or resistance. Whether you laugh instead of cry or cry yourself into a fit of laughter, know that both reactions are valid and serve as important outlets for processing the challenges of divorce.

Day 244

The court system will never give you emotional justice.

The legal process focuses primarily on legal rights, obligations, and fair distribution of assets, often overlooking the intricate emotional dynamics at play. Seeking emotional justice through the court can lead to frustration, disappointment, and an enormous expense as legal outcomes may not align with your deeply felt emotional needs or desires. Instead, seek emotional healing through therapy, support groups, and self-care practices.

Day 245

Be bold and don't allow yourself to play the victim.

Playing the victim often involves relinquishing control and attributing responsibility for your circumstances to external factors. However, by choosing to be bold, you take ownership of your actions and decisions. This mindset shift empowers you to confront challenges head-on, pursue goals with determination, and overcome obstacles with courage and resilience. Being bold encourages you to step out of your comfort zone, seize opportunities, and create the life you want and deserve.

Day 246

*Focus on the positives, and the negatives
will disappear.*

While it's natural to dwell on the negatives of divorce, shifting your focus to the positives can help you heal and move forward. By acknowledging the lessons learned and the growth opportunities that come with adversity, you empower yourself to overcome the pain and embrace a brighter future. Celebrate your strengths, accomplishments, and the relationships that bring joy into your life. Cultivate gratitude for the lessons learned and the new possibilities that lie ahead. Surround yourself with supportive friends and family who uplift and encourage you on your journey. As you focus on the positives, you'll find that the negatives lose their power over you. Instead of dwelling on past hurts, you'll embrace new experiences and build a life filled with happiness, fulfillment, and resilience.

Day 247

Set aside time each week for connecting with friends.

Dedicating time each week to meaningful connections is essential for nurturing your emotional well-being. Opening to trusted confidants about your thoughts and feelings can provide valuable insights, validation, and a feeling of camaraderie. Consider establishing a weekly tradition with a friend that doesn't revolve around your divorce.

Day 248

*Be kind to yourself and don't become a
victim of your circumstances.*

While divorce can bring about immense challenges and
upheaval, allowing yourself to be consumed by a victim
mentality only perpetuates feelings of powerlessness and
despair. Instead, treat yourself with the same kindness and
understanding that you would offer to a dear friend facing
similar circumstances. Remember that your divorce does not
define you; rather, it is but one chapter in the story of your life.

Day 249

*Watch for signs of depression, and
don't wait to get professional help.*

Divorce's emotional toll can show up in various ways, and
symptoms of depression may include ongoing feelings of
sadness, loss of interest in activities you once enjoyed, changes
in appetite or sleep patterns, difficulty concentrating, and
thoughts of hopelessness or worthlessness. Recognizing these
signs early on and seeking help from a therapist or counselor
allows you to explore your emotions, gain perspective, and
develop coping strategies. You don't have to suffer in silence!
Reaching out for help is a courageous and proactive step
toward reclaiming your emotional health and well-being.

Day 250

When life gets super busy and crazy, that's when you must take quiet, still moments for yourself.

While the process of divorce may be fraught with movement and chaos, finding quiet moments can offer a sanctuary for the soul. Inner stillness provides a refuge from the storm, allowing for clarity of thought, emotional balance, and a sense of groundedness amidst uncertainty. Through practices, such as meditation, mindfulness, or simply taking moments of solitude to reconnect with yourself, you can tap into a reservoir of inner peace and strength.

Day 251

The better your mental health, the better your decisions.

By putting your emotional health at the top of your priority list, you are better equipped to navigate the complexities and uncertainties of divorce with clarity, resilience, and sound judgment. Effectively managing stress, anxiety, and other emotional challenges allows you to approach decision-making from a place of strength and stability, rather than falling into impulsive or reactionary behavior. Investing in self-care practices, such as therapy, exercise, mindfulness, and healthy coping mechanisms, not only fosters emotional resilience but also promotes clearer thinking and problem-solving abilities.

Day 252

The cost of divorce is measured by more than just money. There is a huge emotional toll.

The upheaval of separating from a partner, dismantling a shared life, and renegotiating family dynamics can stir up a whirlwind of complex emotions, including grief, anger, guilt, and fear. This emotional journey can be both exhausting and overwhelming, affecting not only both adults but also the children, extended family members, and close friends. This emotional toll can affect individuals for many years post-divorce. Don't be surprised if you experience feelings of loss, shame, or guilt over the breakdown of your marriage resurfacing years later. The important thing to do is recognize the pattern and work to resolve those feelings. By prioritizing self-care, seeking support from loved ones, and perhaps engaging in therapy or counseling, you can navigate the emotional complexities of divorce with greater resilience and emerge stronger and more empowered on the other side.

Day 253

Sometimes, the people around you won't understand your journey. They don't need to; it's not for them.

You don't owe anyone an explanation for the choices you make or the emotions you experience. Your journey through divorce is deeply personal, and only you have the insight and perspective to navigate it authentically. Rather than seeking validation or approval from others, focus on honoring your own truth and prioritizing your well-being.

Day 254

This transformation is painful, but you're not falling apart; you're just falling into something different.

Embracing change can be daunting, but it also holds the promise of growth, resilience, and renewed possibilities. As you navigate this period of transition, trust in your inner strength and resilience to guide you through the challenges and uncertainties. Each step you take toward healing and self-discovery brings you closer to uncovering the depths of your inner beauty and potential. Like a phoenix rising from the ashes, you have the power to emerge from the ashes of divorce with newfound wisdom, grace, and authenticity. Embrace the journey of transformation with courage and openness, knowing that every experience, no matter how painful, contributes to the richness and depth of your being.

Day 255

Try to focus on gratitude, even if your divorce is painful.

Although it may seem difficult, attempting to acknowledge and appreciate the positive aspects of your life, even amidst the pain of divorce, can foster resilience and emotional well-being. Whether it's gratitude for the happy times you shared, the people you met during your marriage, or a new skill or a hobby you embraced, there are a myriad of things you can be grateful for thanks to the time you were married. Also, you can be grateful for the support of loved ones, moments of joy and laughter, or newfound opportunities for growth and self-discovery.

Day 256

Take time to grieve the loss of your relationship.

Whether you initiated the divorce or not, the emotional impact can be profound, evoking a range of complex emotions. Grief is a natural response to loss, and it's essential to honor your feelings and process them in your own time. Allow yourself to acknowledge the sadness, anger, confusion, and even relief that may go with divorce, without judgment or rush. Grieving allows you to come to terms with the end of your marriage, heal emotional wounds, and eventually move forward with clarity and acceptance.

Day 257

Rise above, bite your tongue, take a deep breath
(or a hundred) and be the bigger person.

Choosing to take the high road during divorce entails prioritizing dignity, respect, and integrity in all interactions. Instead of succumbing to bitterness or vindictiveness, opt for compassion, understanding, and cooperation. This means refraining from engaging in petty arguments or seeking revenge, and instead, focusing on finding common ground and working toward an amicable resolution. Taking the high road also involves prioritizing the well-being of any children involved, fostering a supportive co-parenting relationship, and shielding them from unnecessary conflict. While it may not always be easy, rising above the urge to retaliate or escalate conflicts ultimately leads to a more peaceful and constructive divorce process. By demonstrating maturity and grace, you set a positive example for yourself and others, laying the foundation for a healthier post-divorce relationship and paving the way for a brighter future.

Day 258

Maintain your integrity.

Maintaining your integrity throughout the divorce process is paramount. It involves staying true to your values, principles, and moral compass, even amidst the turmoil and emotions. Instead of resorting to deceit, manipulation, or vindictiveness, uphold honesty, transparency, and fairness in all interactions. Keeping your integrity means approaching negotiations with a focus on cooperation and mutual respect, rather than seeking to undermine or discredit the other party. It also entails honoring your commitments and obligations, both legally and ethically, and acting in the best interests of the children involved. By prioritizing integrity, you not only preserve your own self-respect, but also contribute to a more constructive and dignified divorce process. Ultimately, staying true to your principles allows you to navigate the challenges of divorce with grace and honor.

Day 259

If you try to ignore your emotions, it'll only drag out the coping process and come back to haunt you later.

Emotions are a natural and integral part of the divorce experience, and trying to push them aside only delays the inevitable need to confront and process them. By acknowledging and allowing yourself to feel the full spectrum of emotions—whether it's sadness, anger, fear, or relief—you pave the way for genuine healing and growth. Ignoring your emotions may provide temporary relief, but they have a way of resurfacing when least expected, often with greater intensity.

Day 260

Don't waste your beautiful mind on ugly thoughts.

Your mind is a precious asset, capable of resilience and growth, even in the face of adversity. By redirecting your attention toward thoughts of self-compassion, gratitude, and hope, you cultivate a mindset that fosters healing and resilience. Recognize that dwelling on negative thoughts only serves to perpetuate pain and hinder your ability to move forward. Embrace the beauty of your mind by filling it with thoughts that uplift and inspire you. This could be as simple as reading a few pages of an inspiring book, sitting with daily meditation, or taking a walk outside.

Day 261

Keep a sense of humor.

While divorce is undoubtedly a serious and emotionally challenging process, finding reasons to laugh can help ease stress and tension, fostering a more lighthearted perspective on the situation. Whether it's sharing a funny story with a friend, indulging in a favorite comedy, or simply finding humor in the absurdity of certain situations, embracing laughter can be a cathartic release. A sense of humor can remind you that life goes on and that even in the face of adversity, there are moments of joy and levity to be found.

Day 262

Know it's okay to laugh, cry, and everything in between.

Your journey through divorce is unique, and there is no right or wrong way to feel. Allow yourself the space to laugh. Find solace and relief in the humor that life can bring, even during challenging times. Similarly, embrace moments of sadness and tears as part of the healing process, recognizing that they are a natural response to loss and change. By acknowledging and accepting the full spectrum of emotions that go with divorce, you honor your own humanity and pave the way for genuine healing and growth.

Day 263

*Through humor, you can soften some of the
worst blows that life delivers.*

When you infuse moments of humor into not only the divorce process, but life itself, you ease the weight of emotional turmoil. Whether you're sharing lighthearted stories, finding amusement in the absurd, or simply laughing with friends, humor provides a much-needed release valve for your pent-up tension and sorrow. Humor offers a means of coping with the heavy emotions that accompany divorce, allowing you to momentarily set aside your troubles and find comfort in laughter.

Day 264

A feeling fully felt fades.

It may feel uncomfortable, but by allowing yourself to fully experience the depths of your suffering—acknowledging the grief, anger, and sadness that goes with divorce—you will open the door to genuine healing and growth. It's through confronting and processing our pain head-on that you can find peace and resolution. Of course, it would be easier to stick your head in the sand and ignore the emotions, but they will eventually resurface. While the path to healing may be challenging and overwhelming, embracing our suffering with courage and vulnerability leads to a profound transformation.

Day 265

When someone asks how you are doing,
respond by saying, "Better."

During divorce, it's crucial to be mindful of who you confide in. While some individuals genuinely care about your well-being, others may seek gossip. It's wise to avoid sharing information that could harm your case or be used against you. Similarly, it's best to limit sharing with those who have a history of being critical; you don't need that negativity right now. Pay attention to their response; it can reveal whether they're genuinely concerned or just fishing for details. Their reaction will guide you into knowing whether or not you can share more or if it's best to keep certain aspects of your situation private.

Day 266

Learn a few calming breathing techniques.

Whether it's the simple act of deep breathing, more structured practices like diaphragmatic breathing, or the 4-7-8 technique, learning to regulate your breath can have profound effects on your emotional well-being. By focusing on slow, deliberate inhalations and exhalations, you activate the body's relaxation response, reducing levels of stress hormones and promoting a sense of calm. You'll find many options with a simple web search for calming breathing techniques.

Day 267

Don't ignore good nutrition.

If you struggle to eat regular meals, it's okay to listen to your body and opt for alternative sources of nutrition, such as protein shakes. These convenient options provide essential nutrients and energy with no extensive preparation. Prioritizing your physical health can have a profound impact on your ability to cope with the stress and demands of divorce.

Day 268

The cure for anything is saltwater.

Whether it's through the physical exertion of sweat, the emotional release of tears, or the vast expanse of the sea, saltwater serves as a powerful metaphor for the transformative potential inherent in our experiences of pain and loss. Sweating through physical activity can be cathartic, releasing pent-up tension and stress while promoting a sense of vitality and strength. Likewise, allowing yourself to shed tears and express emotions freely can help emotional healing and release, enabling you to process grief and find peace in the release of sorrow. The sea symbolizes the boundless depths of your inner self, offering a metaphorical space for reflection, renewal, and healing. If you don't live near the beach, simply listening to ocean sounds while relaxing can have a similar calming effect.

Day 269

Get outside or open the windows every day.

Making time to connect with the outdoors can offer much-needed solace and rejuvenation for the heart and mind. Whether it's stepping outside for a brisk walk, spending time in a nearby park, or simply opening the windows to let in the cool, crisp air, immersing yourself in nature can have profound benefits for your well-being. Fresh air helps to clear the mind, providing a sense of clarity and perspective.

Day 270

If you're frustrated and angry, take up an exercise class depending on what best suits your mood.

Exercise and movement are amazing healers. Engaging in physical activity, like a boxing class, provides a cathartic release for pent-up emotions, allowing you to release tension and aggression in a controlled environment. The act of punching and kicking can be a powerful metaphor for confronting challenges head-on, empowering you to assert control over your circumstances and find strength in the face of adversity. Alternatively, the gentle movements and mindful breathing of something like tai chi offer a more meditative approach to managing anger, promoting relaxation, inner peace, and emotional balance. Find what your mind and body respond best to, and go for it!

Day 271

Take care of yourself physically, mentally, emotionally, and spiritually so you can be in a better position to make conscious decisions about your future with a calm, clear, rational head.

Taking care of your mental and emotional well-being through practices like therapy, mindfulness, and self-reflection fosters emotional resilience and clarity of thought. Nurturing your spiritual health through activities that nourish your soul and connect you with a sense of purpose can offer solace and guidance during difficult times. Not all three areas may be in balance, so it's important to do a frequent check on which area needs a bit more attention.

Day 272

If you find yourself stress-eating, swap the chocolate for carrots.

While it might not seem as enticing as indulging in chocolate, munching on veggies can offer a satisfying crunch and distraction from emotional triggers. You can always add a bit of peanut butter to celery or dip carrots in ranch dressing. So, next time stress-eating tempts you, reach for the veggies—they might not be glamorous, but they'll provide a healthy alternative.

Day 273

Find healthy outlets for stress.

While it may be tempting to turn to binge-eating, alcohol, or drugs to cope, these behaviors exacerbate feelings of despair and hinder the healing process. Instead, focus on finding constructive ways to ease stress and promote well-being. Engaging in physical activity, such as walking, jogging, or yoga, can help release tension and boost your mood by triggering the release of endorphins, the body's natural stress relievers. Connecting with supportive friends and family members or joining a support group can provide invaluable emotional support and validation during this challenging time.

Day 274

Movement is good for the soul.

Scheduling time on your calendar for exercise, whether it's a simple walk around the block or a kickboxing class, can be a powerful tool for nurturing your well-being during this challenging time. Engaging in movement releases endorphins, which are natural mood boosters, helping to alleviate stress, anxiety, and depression that often go with divorce. Exercise also offers a much-needed outlet for pent-up emotions, providing a healthy means of processing feelings of anger, frustration, or sadness. Whether it's the rhythmic pounding of feet on the pavement or the exhilaration of a high-energy workout, movement has the power to ground us in the present.

Day 275

Give your mind a break. Read a chapter of a favorite book ... or a book of total fluff.

Whether it's immersing yourself in a chapter of a favorite book or delving into the pages of a light-hearted novel filled with fluffy entertainment, reading offers a respite from the seriousness of divorce. Engaging with literature allows you to step outside of your own reality for a while, losing yourself in captivating stories, intriguing characters, and imaginative worlds. Joining a book club might be a good option as well.

Day 276

You must refuel yourself often. If you run on empty for too long, your body will break down.

Just like a car requires fuel to keep running smoothly, your mind, body, and spirit also need nourishment to withstand the demands of this challenging journey. Ignoring your own needs and running on empty for too long can lead to emotional burnout and breakdown. Whether it's taking a leisurely walk in nature, indulging in a hobby you love, or simply practicing mindfulness and relaxation techniques, make self-care a non-negotiable priority. Remember, you cannot pour from an empty cup, so prioritize self-care as an essential step toward navigating divorce with strength and grace.

Day 277

To improve your outlook, keep looking up!

The simple act of looking up, whether it's gazing at the sky, admiring the beauty of nature, or seeking inspiration from uplifting quotes, can help shift your perspective and cultivate a sense of optimism. By directing your gaze toward the heavens, you're reminded of the vastness of the world beyond your immediate circumstances, offering a sense of perspective and possibility. It's a subtle yet profound reminder that even in the darkest moments, there is light to be found, and hope to be nurtured.

Day 278

Don't suffer in silence.

If you feel blue or overwhelmed, reach out and talk to someone you trust. Suffering in silence only intensifies feelings of isolation and despair. However, opening up allows for connection, understanding, and validation. Talking to someone not only helps you feel heard and supported, but also offers perspective and insight into your situation. This could be a trusted friend, counselor, or even your dog. Sometimes, it's the simple act of speaking your emotions out loud that brings a sense of relief. Remember, seeking help is a sign of strength, not weakness.

Day 279

Take all the time you need to heal emotionally. Moving on consists of many tiny steps; not one giant leap.

Moving on is a gradual process that involves taking small, incremental steps toward acceptance and healing. Each step, no matter how small, brings you closer to reclaiming your sense of self and finding peace amidst the turmoil. Whether it's allowing yourself to grieve the loss of your marriage, seeking support from loved ones, or engaging in activities that bring you joy and fulfillment, every action contributes to your emotional well-being. Remember, healing is not linear; there will be good days and bad days, moments of progress, and moments of setbacks. Be patient and compassionate with yourself as you navigate this journey of self-discovery and renewal.

Day 280

*Set aside ten minutes a day for meditation,
preferably in the morning.*

Meditation offers a sanctuary from the chaos of daily life, allowing you to center yourself and ground your mind amidst the swirling emotions and uncertainties of divorce. Even if it's just ten minutes early in the day, you can practice mindfulness techniques such as focused breathing or body scanning, gently guiding your awareness back to the present moment whenever your thoughts wander. Through consistent practice, meditation strengthens your ability to remain calm and centered in the face of adversity, fostering a sense of inner peace and stability that transcends external circumstances. If you're new to meditation, do a web search for guided meditations.

PS: If meditating at home is too distracting, go for a walk and sit quietly on a bench or take a ride and sit in your car.

Day 281

Self-guided meditation can help clear your head and put a positive spin on the day.

Embracing self-guided meditation can serve as a powerful tool for mental clarity and emotional well-being. Taking time each day to engage in this practice allows you to quiet the noise of your mind and cultivate a sense of inner peace. By focusing your attention inward, you can release stress, anxiety, and negative thought patterns, creating space for positivity to flourish. Self-guided meditation offers an opportunity to reframe your perspective and shift toward a more optimistic outlook on the day ahead. Through intentional breathing exercises, visualization techniques, or guided affirmations, you can redirect your thoughts to gratitude, resilience, and self-empowerment.

Day 282

*Meditation, yoga, listening to music, or deep
breathing are simple ways to relieve stress.*

Meditation allows you to quiet the incessant chatter of your thoughts and cultivate a state of mindfulness, enabling you to see your emotions without becoming overwhelmed by them. Similarly, practicing yoga offers a holistic approach to stress relief, combining gentle movement, breathwork, and mindfulness to release tension and promote relaxation. Listening to music can have a profound impact on your mood, transporting you to a place of comfort and solace. Even the simple act of taking deep, intentional breaths can signal to your body that it's safe to relax, activating the parasympathetic nervous system and reducing levels of stress hormones.

Day 283

If you feel overwhelmed or angry, find a release.

When the weight of divorce becomes overwhelming or emotions like anger threaten to engulf you, it's crucial to seek healthy outlets for release and support before you blow your stack. The important thing is to acknowledge when you're near the breaking point and take positive action.

Day 284

Weed out negative people.

Negative people and friends can drain your energy, amplify feelings of self-doubt, and hinder your healing and renewal progress. Therefore, it's important to prioritize relationships that nourish your soul and contribute to your growth. This may involve setting boundaries with toxic individuals or gradually distancing yourself from negative influences. While it may seem daunting, keeping your circle tight and positive is a necessary step to creating a supportive environment, which is critical to your emotional recovery. Once you're in a good place, you can intentionally choose to expand your circle and only let in those who contribute positively to your new chapter.

Day 285

When someone you trust asks how you are doing, have a response ready that does not mask your struggles and opens the door for compassion.

When someone in your trusted inner circle asks how you are doing, consider crafting a response that acknowledges your emotions and opens the door for meaningful connection. For instance, you might say, "I'm taking it one day at a time, and some days are harder than others. But I'm grateful for the support of friends like you." This response allows you to express your vulnerability while also highlighting the importance of support and empathy.

Divorce Mess to Happiness

Day 286

*You need to look ahead, but don't look too far,
as it can be overwhelming.*

Strive for a balance between planning for the future and staying grounded in the here and now. Focus on setting short-term goals that are manageable and realistic, rather than getting caught up in the distant possibilities of the future. By breaking down the journey into smaller, more manageable steps, you can ease some of the overwhelm and maintain a sense of control over your circumstances.

Day 287

*Everything shifts when you replace, "Why is this
happening to me?" with "What is this teaching me?"*

During divorce, shifting your perspective from asking, "Why is this happening to me?" to "What is this teaching me?" can bring about a profound transformation in your mindset and approach to the situation. By seeking the lessons and insights that divorce offers, you empower yourself to extract meaning from the challenges you face and emerge stronger and more resilient on the other side. It invites you to embrace the journey of self-exploration and personal growth that divorce presents, recognizing that even amidst the pain and upheaval, there are valuable lessons to be learned. Remember, you are the hero of your own life, so do not become the victim.

Day 288

The first to forgive is the strongest;
the first to forget is the happiest.

By extending forgiveness, you release the burden of carrying grudges and grievances, freeing yourself from the emotional weight of the past. Being the first to forget, to move beyond the pain and embrace a future unburdened by bitterness, welcomes a newfound sense of happiness and liberation. It signifies a willingness to release the grip of past hurts and embrace the possibilities of the present moment and beyond. While forgiving and forgetting may not come easily, they are transformative acts of self-love and empowerment.

Day 289

Life's too short to waste time hating anyone.

Recognize that holding onto hatred only weighs you down and prevents you from fully embracing the beauty and potential of life. Every moment spent in bitterness is a moment lost to the possibility of joy, love, and fulfillment. By letting go of grudges and choosing to move forward with an open heart, you liberate yourself from the shackles of negativity and create space for peace and healing to flourish. Embrace the present moment with gratitude and an unwavering commitment to positivity, knowing that life's too short to waste on animosity and resentment.

Day 290

*Try to ensure your divorce does not
negatively affect the rest of your life.*

While divorce can be a deeply challenging experience, it's important not to allow it to define or dictate the course of your life. Instead, focus on empowering yourself to overcome adversity and embrace the opportunities for growth and renewal that lie ahead. Remember, while divorce may mark the end of one chapter, it also signifies the beginning of a new journey filled with endless possibilities. With determination, resilience, and self-love, you can rise above the challenges of divorce and create a future that is defined by strength, joy, and fulfillment.

Day 291

Avoid seeking revenge.

The temptation to seek revenge for being wronged may feel overwhelming, fueled by feelings of anger, betrayal, and hurt. However, succumbing to this impulse only perpetuates a cycle of negativity and prolongs the pain for both of you. Instead, work hard to rise above the desire for retaliation and focus on fostering healing and personal growth. Recognize that seeking revenge will not bring you the closure or satisfaction you crave. What is one thing you secretly desire revenge on, but know you should release and move on from?

Day 292

*Believe in yourself, and don't let this
one incident bring you down.*

Believe in yourself and your ability to overcome adversity, recognizing that divorce does not define your worth or dictate your destiny. While the pain may feel intense in the present moment, it is temporary, and you have the power to shape your own narrative. Embrace the opportunity for growth and transformation that divorce presents, using it as a catalyst to discover your true strength and resilience. Know that setbacks are a natural part of life's journey.

Day 293

*For every minute you are angry, you lose
sixty seconds of happiness.*

With each passing minute spent consumed by bitterness and resentment, precious moments of happiness slip away unnoticed. By releasing the grip of anger, you reclaim your own happiness and empower yourself to embrace the present moment with openness and positivity. Redirect your energy toward whatever brings you joy and fulfillment, refusing to let anger overshadow the beauty of life's simple pleasures. Remember, while anger may feel justified in the moment, its long-term consequences far outweigh any temporary satisfaction it may bring.

Day 294

*If you feel like you're going through Hell, don't
stop until you get to the other side.*

Rather than falling victim to despair or allowing yourself to
become paralyzed by the challenges you face, keep pushing
forward with unwavering determination and courage. Each
step you take, no matter how small, brings you one step closer
to finding light on the other side. Trust in your inner strength
and resilience, knowing that you have the power to overcome
even the most daunting of obstacles. Above all, hold on to hope
and the belief that brighter days are ahead.

Day 295

*Don't confuse your path with your destination. Just
because you are in the middle of a storm now doesn't
mean sunshine isn't heading your way.*

While the journey may be fraught with obstacles and
uncertainties, it's essential to remember that they are merely
temporary setbacks on the path to your ultimate goals. Like a
passing storm, the difficulties you meet along the way will
eventually give way to brighter days and opportunities for
growth. By staying focused on our long-term aspirations and
staying resilient in the face of adversity, you can navigate
through life's storms with grace and determination.

Day 296

*Be ready for a drastic and surprising
change in your friendships.*

Some friendships may grow stronger as friends rally around you for support. However, you may also experience a shift in your social circle, with some friends distancing themselves or choosing sides. This can be unexpected and even hurtful, especially if you count on certain friendships for support. It's essential to be prepared for these changes and understand that they are a natural part of the divorce process. While it may be disappointing to see some friendships fade away, it can also create space for new connections and opportunities to cultivate healthier relationships. Keep focusing on nurturing friendships that bring positivity and support into your life.

Day 297

Pretending to be strong is exhausting.

You're going to have a lot of emotions coming and going during divorce and it's essential to acknowledge them. Suppressing your emotions can lead to increased stress and mental health issues. Instead of bottling up your feelings, permit yourself to express them openly and honestly. If you need to cry, let the tears flow without shame or guilt. Crying is a natural and healthy way to release pent-up emotions and process your grief. Remember, it's okay to not always be strong.

Day 298

It's natural to feel lost. Just be sure to have friends who can pull you out of your funk.

Suddenly, uncertainty and upheaval replace the familiar routines that once defined daily life. It's natural to feel lost as you navigate the unfamiliar territory and adjust to a new reality, but it's important not to allow yourself to become consumed by this sense of loss and disorientation. Reach out to friends and loved ones who can provide support. Surrounding yourself with a strong support network can offer comfort, perspective, and practical help as you rebuild your life.

Day 299

Even if the divorce is quick, healing takes time.

While the legal process of divorce may conclude relatively quickly, the emotional healing that follows can be a prolonged journey. It's essential for you to give yourself permission to grieve the end of your marriage and acknowledge the complex array of emotions that accompany it. Healing from divorce requires time, patience, and self-compassion. It involves processing the pain and trauma of the past while gradually rebuilding a sense of identity and purpose. Each person's healing journey is unique, and there is no set timeline for moving forward.

Day 300

Healing doesn't mean the damage never existed; it means the damage no longer controls you.

Healing after divorce is a complex and deeply personal journey. It involves acknowledging the pain and trauma of the past while actively working toward emotional and psychological recovery. This process doesn't erase the scars or the memories of the past, but it empowers you to transcend pain and reclaim control over your life. Healing is about finding inner strength and resilience, releasing the grip of past hurts, and moving forward with renewed purpose and vitality. It requires confronting difficult emotions, such as anger, grief, and resentment, and embracing self-compassion and forgiveness.

Day 301

Make peace with your past; don't screw up the present.

Holding onto resentment, anger, or regret from past relationships can hinder your ability to move forward and make the most of your current circumstances. By acknowledging and accepting the past, you can release yourself from its grip and focus on creating a positive and fulfilling present. This involves letting go of any lingering emotional baggage, forgiving yourself and others for past mistakes, and embracing the opportunity for growth and transformation.

Day 302

Anxiety comes from the desire to control the future.

It's important to recognize that most anxiety stems not from actual events but from the desire to manipulate and shape outcomes according to expectations. The realization that you cannot control every aspect of your life can unsettle you, but it also presents an opportunity for liberation. By relinquishing the illusion of control, you can find a sense of peace amidst the chaos. Instead of trying to dictate the course of events, you can focus on cultivating resilience, adaptability, and acceptance.

Day 303

No matter how much it hurts right now, one day you'll look back and realize it changed your life for the better.

It's often said that time heals all wounds. While the healing process may be slow and difficult, it's important to hold on to the belief that brighter days lie ahead. When you look back, the tumultuous journey through divorce may reveal itself as a catalyst for profound personal growth and transformation. Adversity has a way of shaping us, molding us into stronger, more resilient versions of ourselves. What feels like the end of the road may, in fact, be the beginning of a new chapter filled with unforeseen opportunities and blessings. So, while the pain may be excruciating in the present moment, it's essential to maintain faith in the possibility of a brighter tomorrow.

Chapter 8
From Surviving to Thriving: Moving on with Peace and Purpose

Day 304

Nothing will screw up today more than an unresolved past.

By making peace with the past, you free yourself from the burdens of bitterness and regret, creating space for healing, growth, and renewal in your life. Embrace the opportunity to let go of old wounds and release the emotional baggage that may weigh you down, allowing yourself to embrace the present moment with openness and positivity. If you don't acknowledge and address the reasons for the breakdown in your marriage, you may be ripe for repeating the behaviors in your next relationship. Redirect your energy toward cultivating positivity and resilience, nurturing your own well-being, and building a future filled with hope and possibility.

Day 305

*Don't let the person who didn't love you
keep you from the person who will.*

By letting go of the person who didn't love you, you create space in your heart for someone who will embrace you with open arms and genuine affection. Focus your energy on nurturing your own well-being and self-worth, surrounding yourself with positivity and individuals who uplift and support your journey. Once you have healed from the pain of divorce, trust in the power of love to transcend past disappointments and lead you to the person who will cherish and value you as you deserve. Remember, you are worthy of love and happiness.

Day 306

Don't ruin today by thinking about a bad yesterday.

Dwelling on yesterday's hardships can spoil the beauty of today. Instead of allowing past hurts to consume you, focus on the opportunities and joys of the present moment. By shifting your mindset away from negative thoughts about yesterday, you free yourself to fully embrace the possibilities of today. Every day is a new chance to find happiness, growth, and fulfillment, even amidst the challenges of divorce. So, don't let the shadows of yesterday dim the brightness of today. Choose to live in the present, where hope and resilience can flourish, guiding you toward a brighter tomorrow.

Day 307

There is peace in letting go.

Though it may seem daunting, releasing the grip on what once was can lead to a sense of inner peace. Letting go doesn't mean forgetting or denying the pain; rather, it's about acknowledging the reality of the situation and accepting it for what it is. By relinquishing the need to control outcomes or hold on to the past, you create space for healing and growth. Embracing the concept of letting go allows you to redirect your energy toward building a new future for yourself.

Day 308

Be brave enough to say goodbye, and
life will give you something new.

Saying goodbye to parts of your past can be the hardest decision you'll ever make, but it's also a powerful act of bravery. As you summon the strength to let go, you allow space for new beginnings and fresh opportunities to enter your life. Though the road ahead may seem uncertain, trust that life has a way of rewarding bravery with unexpected hellos. With each goodbye, you make space for growth, resilience, and transformation. While the journey through divorce may be challenging, it also holds the promise of renewal and hope. So, dare to be brave in your goodbyes, knowing that life's next hello awaits with open arms, ready to lead you toward a brighter tomorrow.

Day 309

Don't dwell on the past.

Instead of dwelling on the pain of separation, choose to focus on the blessings and joys that the relationship brought into your life. Reflect on the lessons learned, the growth experienced, and the love shared, knowing that each moment, whether joyful or challenging, contributed to your journey of self-discovery and personal growth. Embrace the beauty of the memories and smile knowing that love, in all its forms, is a precious gift that enriches our lives in profound ways.

Day 310

You will be a different person when you emerge from this storm.

Just as a storm leaves its mark on the landscape, divorce leaves an indelible imprint on the psyche, reshaping beliefs, priorities, and aspirations. The person you are walking into the storm may feel battered and broken. The person you are when emerging on the other side is transformed, forged anew by the fires of adversity. You will carry the scars of battle, but also the lessons learned, the growth experienced, and the newfound sense of self-awareness and empowerment that comes from facing your darkest fears head-on.

Day 311

Get real with your finances; live within your means.

Inspect your income, expenses, and overall financial health to gain a clear understanding of where you stand. Be realistic about what you can afford and prioritize living within your means. This may require adjusting your lifestyle and spending habits to ensure financial stability both during and after the divorce process. Whenever possible, do not become dependent upon child or spousal support. You will have peace of mind if you can meet your financial commitments without relying on your former spouse.

Day 312

Surrender to self-discovery and reconnect with your true self.

People who divorce often report having lost a piece of themselves while married. Divorce can prompt a period of introspection and self-exploration, as you rediscover and reassess your priorities, values, and goals. It's through this journey of self-discovery that you can cultivate a deeper understanding of your genuine needs, laying the foundation for healthy relationships in the future. By prioritizing self-awareness and self-care, you can emerge from divorce with a renewed sense of independence and empowerment, ready to embrace life on your own terms.

Day 313

With the right perspective, wounds are wisdom.

While divorce can leave emotional scars and wounds that may seem insurmountable at first, embracing a positive perspective can transform these challenges into opportunities for growth and insight. What initially may have seemed like irreparable damage can evolve into wisdom, guiding you toward healthier choices and behaviors in the future. By reframing your perspective and viewing divorce as a catalyst for personal growth and transformation, you will emerge from the experience stronger, wiser, and more resilient than before.

Day 314

When you forgive, you change the future.

Forgiveness liberates you from the shackles of resentment, bitterness, and anger, allowing you to release the weight of past grievances and move forward with a renewed sense of freedom and clarity. By relinquishing the need to hold on to past hurts, you create space for healing, reconciliation, and new beginnings. It enables you to cultivate healthier relationships, set boundaries, and make empowered choices that align with your values and aspirations. Ultimately, forgiveness is a courageous act of self-love and liberation, empowering you to reclaim agency over your life and embrace the possibilities of a brighter, more hopeful future.

Day 315

Don't use the past as an excuse to miss out on your future.

Clinging to past hurts as an excuse to avoid moving forward only limits your growth and happiness. Instead of allowing the past to hold you back, use it as a springboard for personal evolution. Reflect on the lessons learned from your divorce and let them guide you toward a brighter future. Embrace the opportunity to rewrite your story, free from the constraints of past mistakes and regrets. By letting go of the past, you open yourself up to new experiences, relationships, and possibilities that await you. Don't allow the pain of divorce to define your future; instead, let it inspire you to create a life filled with joy, fulfillment, and purpose.

Day 316

You are not stuck unless you decide to be.

While you may feel you're trapped in a state of limbo, you hold the power to shape your own destiny. You are not bound by the limitations of your current situation unless you choose to be. By taking steps to chart an alternative course for yourself, you can break free from the chains of the past and create a future filled with hope, happiness, and fulfillment. Remember, you are the author of your own story, and your potential is limitless.

Day 317

*Being with no one is better than being with
the wrong one.*

During and after divorcing, you may feel lonely, adrift, and grappling with the uncertainty of what comes next. While you may feel tempted to jump into another relationship to fill the loneliness, it's important to remember that a toxic or unsatisfying relationship only feeds into unhappiness and stifles personal growth. The prospect of being alone may seem daunting at first, but it presents an opportunity for you to rediscover your inner strength and resilience. During this time, you will learn to rely on your own instincts and judgment, developing a sense of independence. In the end, being alone becomes not a source of fear, but a badge of courage and a symbol of liberation from unhealthy relationships.

Day 318

Forgiveness is a daily choice.

Forgiveness is not a onetime event, but rather, a daily choice that requires ongoing commitment and effort. Each time you choose to forgive, you release the emotional weight of the past and create space for healing and renewal. Forgiveness is a process, not a destination, and each time you choose to forgive, you take a step closer to healing.

Day 319

Don't start your day with the broken pieces of yesterday.

Embrace each morning as an opportunity for fresh beginnings and new possibilities. Take a moment to acknowledge the emotions and experiences of the past, but don't allow them to overshadow the potential for growth and healing in the present moment. Choose to let go of regrets, grievances, and negative thoughts that may weigh you down, and instead focus on the opportunities for growth and transformation that lie ahead. Each new day offers a fresh opportunity to rewrite your story and create the life you deserve.

Day 320

Never change so people like you.

Instead of compromising your values or identity to please others, embrace your true self and trust that the right people will appreciate and love you for who you are. By staying true to yourself, you attract individuals who appreciate your authenticity and share your values, creating deeper and more fulfilling connections. You are worthy of love and acceptance just as you are, and by embracing your true self, you invite genuine connections and meaningful relationships into your life. Stay true to yourself, follow your heart, and trust that the right people will love and appreciate the real you.

Day 321

Clean up one mess before you make another.

Rather than allowing problems to accumulate, prioritize addressing them one by one, methodically cleaning up each mess before it has the chance to escalate. Whether it's resolving legal matters, organizing finances, establishing a co-parenting plan, or even doing a load of laundry, tackling each issue as it arises ensures that you're not overwhelmed by the weight of unresolved issues. Addressing problems as they come up prevents them from snowballing into larger and more daunting challenges down the line. This also goes for starting a new romantic relationship. Give yourself time to fully heal from your marriage before you jump in with someone new.

Day 322

It's better to remain single while maintaining high standards than to be in a relationship and settle for less than you deserve.

While the prospect of being single may initially seem daunting, settling for a relationship that falls short of your standards can ultimately lead to dissatisfaction and unhappiness. Instead of compromising on your values or wants out of fear of being alone, embrace the opportunity to prioritize your well-being and fulfillment. Trust in your worth and the importance of honoring your needs and aspirations.

Day 323

One of the hardest but most important things in life is learning to let go and trust that there is a lesson in everything that happens.

Divorce forces you to confront one of life's toughest lessons: the art of letting go and finding meaning in every experience. It's a journey marked by pain, uncertainty, and profound introspection; however, every challenge carries with it an opportunity for growth and learning. Though it may be difficult to see the silver lining amidst the storm, trust that there is wisdom to be gained from every twist and turn of your journey. Embrace the lessons that divorce offers, whether it's discovering newfound strength within yourself, learning to prioritize your happiness, or gaining clarity about your values and aspirations. Allow yourself to release the grip of bitterness and resentment, and instead, cultivate an attitude of openness and acceptance. By embracing the lessons of the past, you pave the way for healing, transformation, and a brighter future. Trust in the inherent wisdom of life's experiences, knowing that each setback is merely a stepping stone on the path to personal growth and fulfillment.

Day 324

Let go of past hurts. Free yourself up for
an awesome future!

Embrace the opportunity to free yourself from the burden of carrying old wounds, allowing yourself to step into a future filled with hope, possibility, and joy. Redirect your focus toward cultivating positivity and resilience, nurturing your well-being, and pursuing goals and aspirations that align with your values and dreams. Surround yourself with supportive individuals who uplift and encourage you on your journey, and trust in your ability to overcome adversity and create the life you want. Remember, the past does not define you, and by releasing its hold on your present, you empower yourself to embrace the limitless potential of the future with open arms and a hopeful heart.

Day 325

You know all those things you've always
wanted to do? Go do them.

Perhaps during your marriage, there were hobbies or interests that you set on the back burner. Now is the time to bring them to the front, and these are the words that serve as a rallying cry to go forth and chase after the things that set your soul on fire, for the world is yours to explore and conquer.

Day 326

Without standards, you'll settle for anything.

Divorce often prompts a period of self-discovery and redefinition, offering an opportunity to rise above adversity and become the person you were meant to be. Establishing and supporting personal standards sets the foundation for a future filled with authenticity and fulfillment. Instead of compromising on your values or settling for relationships and situations that do not align with your vision, use divorce as a catalyst for personal growth. By rising above the challenges and adhering to your standards, you not only honor your self-worth but also attract the connections and experiences that align with your true desires into your life.

Day 327

You can't start the next chapter of your life
if you keep reading the last one.

By fixating on the past, you risk becoming trapped in a cycle of regret and stagnation, preventing you from embracing the potential for growth and renewal in the present moment. Instead of dwelling on what could have been or what went wrong, focus your energy on creating a new narrative for yourself—one that is defined by resilience, optimism, and possibility. Embrace the lessons learned from the past, but don't allow them to dictate the trajectory of your future.

Day 327

When you ignore your past, it controls you. But when you embrace your past, you get to shape your future.

You are going to face a choice: either deny the reality of your experience or embrace it wholeheartedly. Denying your story only allows it to wield power over you, shaping your identity and influencing your future in ways you may not intend. However, when you take ownership of your story, you reclaim control over your narrative and empower yourself to shape its outcome. By acknowledging the pain, the challenges, and the lessons learned from your divorce, you gain the ability to write the ending you desire. It's a journey of self-discovery and empowerment, where you refuse to be defined by past struggles and instead use them as fuel for growth and transformation. It's not about erasing the chapters of your past, but rather, integrating them into a narrative of resilience, courage, and hope.

Day 328

Start your own traditions.

Intentionally creating new rituals and customs allows you to reclaim a sense of ownership over your life. Whether it's celebrating holidays in a new way, establishing weekly rituals with your children, or starting personal traditions that bring you joy, the possibilities are endless. By starting your own traditions, you redefine what family and celebration mean to you, honoring the past while embracing the future with hope and optimism. These new traditions serve as a reminder that life goes on and that with each new tradition, you are actively shaping the narrative of your post-divorce journey.

Day 329

You know what it's like to see love slip away, and you're more able to keep it from happening again.

The pain of seeing love slip away serves as a powerful reminder of the fragility of. Armed with this knowledge, you are likely equipped to better recognize the warning signs of trouble in a relationship and take proactive steps to address them before it is too late. You understand the value of prioritizing emotional intimacy, mutual respect, and compromise in a partnership, and are more willing to invest the time and effort needed to cultivate a strong and lasting connection.

Day 330

Don't fear falling apart; it's a chance to rebuild yourself into the person you've always wanted to be.

Rather than fearing the process of falling apart, embrace it as an opportunity for growth, self-discovery, and renewal. Divorce can be a catalyst for profound personal transformation, offering a chance to reassess priorities, values, and aspirations. Instead of clinging to the remnants of a past life, view the experience as a blank canvas upon which you can paint a new and empowered version of yourself. Use this opportunity to rebuild yourself in alignment with the person you've always wanted to be—strong, resilient, and true to your authentic self. Remember, the seeds of a powerful breakthrough lie in every breakdown, and by embracing the opportunity to rebuild yourself, you unlock the possibility of a life filled with purpose, authenticity, and joy.

Day 331

*The only thing harder than walking away is
not looking back.*

Parting ways from marriage is undeniably challenging. Yet, perhaps even more daunting is resisting the temptation to glance back, to linger in what once was. Like a magnetic pull, memories and emotions tug at the heartstrings, urging a backward glance. However, forging ahead requires a steadfast resolve to keep your gaze fixed on the horizon of possibility rather than dwelling in the shadows of the past. It's like embarking on a journey toward self-discovery, where each step forward signifies a conscious choice to embrace the unknown.

Day 332

Reflect and understand what makes you truly happy.

Instead of allowing yourself to be consumed by the chaos and emotions of the moment, carve out dedicated time for reflection and introspection. Ask yourself questions about your passions, interests, and sources of joy. Explore activities and experiences that ignite a sense of purpose and meaning within you. Embrace the opportunity to reconnect with your authentic self and honor your innermost desires and aspirations. True happiness comes from living authentically and aligning your life with your deepest values and aspirations.

Day 333

It might be better, or it might just be different.

It's natural to wonder whether life beyond divorce will be better or merely different. The truth is, there are no guarantees. What lies ahead may bring newfound freedom, growth, and happiness, but it may also present its own set of challenges and adjustments. It's a journey marked by ambiguity and complexity, where the outcomes are as varied as the individuals involved. Rather than fixating on the elusive notion of "okay," focus on embracing the changes and opportunities that lie before you. Embrace the chance to rediscover yourself, cultivate new relationships, and pursue passions and dreams that you may have sidelined in the past. Ultimately, whether life post-divorce is better or simply different is a matter of perspective. It's about finding contentment and fulfillment in the present moment, regardless of the challenges and uncertainties that may arise.

Day 334

You've got a few scars. They make you more interesting.

Instead of viewing your emotional scars as blemishes to be hidden or ashamed of, embrace them as badges of honor that illustrate your journey through adversity. Just like a blacksmith polishes and refines a piece of silver through the process of forging, the challenges you've faced shape and strengthen you. Your scars are a testament to your courage, perseverance, and strength in the face of hardship. They make you more than just interesting; they make you uniquely beautiful and resilient.

Day 335

If you were happy with the wrong one, just think how happy you will be when the right one comes along.

While it may be tempting to dwell on the mistakes of the past, it's important to maintain hope for the future and trust in the possibility of finding love again, once you emotionally heal and feel ready. Being happy with the wrong person is not a reflection of your worth or potential for happiness, but rather, a steppingstone on the path to finding the right one. Trust in the timing of your life and have faith that the right person will come along when you're ready. Focus on healing and nurturing yourself in the meantime, and remain open to the possibility of love in all its forms.

Day 337

With each obstacle you overcome, you are stronger.

The process of divorce forces you to confront your deepest fears and insecurities, pushing you to develop coping mechanisms and strategies for managing difficult emotions. With each trial and tribulation, you emerge stronger, more self-aware, and better equipped to navigate the ups and downs of life. Rather than succumbing to despair or allowing yourself to be defined by pain, harness your well of inner strength and resilience to forge a path forward. Lean on your support systems, draw strength from all experiences empowers you to face whatever challenges come your way.

Day 338

Swap criticism for self-love.

Embrace your flaws and imperfections as part of what makes you beautifully human, worthy of love and acceptance. Shift your focus from self-criticism to self-appreciation, acknowledging your strengths, resilience, and the unique qualities that make you who you are. Remember, you are deserving of love, both from others and from yourself, and by embracing self-love.

Day 339

Starting over is not all that bad because when you restart, you get another chance to make things better.

With each new beginning comes the chance to learn from past mistakes, grow from experiences, and make choices that align with your authentic self. Embrace the journey of starting over with courage, resilience, and an open heart, knowing that with each step forward, you are moving closer to a life that reflects your genuine desires and aspirations. Remember, starting over is not a sign of failure, but rather, a testament to your strength and resilience in the face of adversity.

Day 340

Healing takes time.

It's natural to yearn for a quick fix, hoping that one day, you'll wake up with a heart miraculously healed from the pain and anguish of divorce. However, healing is not a linear process, and expecting an overnight transformation can lead to disappointment and frustration. Instead of fixating on the idea of a healed heart, shift your focus toward living a full and meaningful life, even with a broken one. Recognize that healing takes time and patience, and there is no shame in carrying a broken heart as you navigate through life's challenges.

Day 341

Be in love with your life.

Embrace being in love with your life, cherishing every minute, regardless of the challenges you may face. Find moments of beauty and grace in every day. Allow yourself to revel in the small pleasures and joys that surround you, recognizing that even amidst the chaos of divorce, there is still much to be grateful for. Embrace the journey of self-discovery and growth, knowing that every experience, both joyful and painful, contributes to the richness and depth of your life.

Day 342

Most people have more than one soulmate.

While society often romanticizes the idea of finding "the one," most people have more than one soulmate throughout their lifetime. A soulmate is not necessarily a romantic partner, but someone who deeply understands and connects with your innermost self on a profound level. These soul connections can manifest in various forms, including friendships, familial relationships, and even fleeting encounters with strangers. Each soulmate brings their own unique gifts, lessons, and opportunities for growth into your life, enriching your journey with their presence and influence.

Day 343

To forgive is the highest, most beautiful form of love.

While forgiveness may not come easily, it is a transformative process that offers liberation from the bonds of bitterness and pain. By choosing to forgive, you reclaim your power, refusing to allow past hurts to define your present and future. In return for this act of grace, you open yourself up to a world of infinite possibilities where peace and happiness abound.

Day 344

You can't change the past, but you can begin from this moment to create a fresh and different ending.

Divorce marks the end of one chapter in life but also signals the beginning of a new journey filled with endless possibilities. Despite the pain and heartache of the past, each day presents an opportunity to start anew, to rewrite the narrative of our lives, and to create a brand-new ending. It means embracing the present moment with gratitude and intention, knowing that every choice and action has the power to shape the course of our lives. By focusing on the here and now, you reclaim your authorship over your own story, empowered to create a future filled with hope, love, and fulfillment.

Day 345

What lies ahead is far better than what we leave behind.

While it's easy to fixate on what you have lost, focusing on the possibilities that lie ahead allows you to embrace the future with hope and optimism. By letting go of the past and looking forward with anticipation, you open yourself up to the possibility of experiencing joy, fulfillment, and love in ways you never imagined. Each day presents a new opportunity to chart your own path, pursue your dreams, and create a life that aligns with your deepest desires and aspirations.

Day 346

Life always offers you a second chance,
which is called tomorrow.

Each day brings with it the opportunity for renewal and growth; a chance to rewrite your story and pursue the life you truly desire. It's about finding strength in the face of adversity and refusing to be defined by past mistakes or setbacks. It's about embracing the endless potential of tomorrow and seizing the opportunity to create a brighter, more fulfilling future. Tomorrow offers us the chance to start anew and build the life we've always dreamed of.

Day 347

What happened yesterday no longer matters.

Dwelling on yesterday's hardships serves no purpose in navigating the path forward. What transpired yesterday, whether it be moments of sorrow, regret, or heartache, no longer rules the present or the future. Instead, it's about embracing the here and now, seizing each moment as an opportunity for growth, healing, and renewal. While the scars of the past may linger, they do not define who you are or dictate the course of your life. Embrace the blank canvas of the future as you turn the page, filled with hope, courage, and optimism.

Day 348

Time is better spent building something new.

Instead of letting bitterness or regret take over during divorce, accept the chance to start anew. By directing your efforts toward building a future filled with possibility and promise, you reclaim your own life. It's about releasing yourself from the past and stepping boldly into the unknown, knowing that you have the power to shape your own destiny. Be inspired to cultivate a mindset of resilience, creativity, and optimism as you embark on a journey of self-discovery and renewal. Change is not to be feared, but rather, embraced as a doorway to new opportunities, experiences, and possibilities.

Day 349

Let your past fuel future adventures.

In the wake of divorce, it's easy to become tethered to the pain and regrets of the past, allowing them to overshadow the potential for new beginnings. However, these words are a powerful reminder that our past experiences, no matter how painful, can serve as catalysts for growth and transformation. Rather than allowing the weight of past hardships to hold you back, you can harness them as fuel for future adventures. With each step forward, you reclaim our ownership over your story, empowered to create a future that is rich in adventure, fulfillment, and joy.

Day 350

Love when you're ready, not when you're lonely.

Rushing into a new relationship before you have had the chance to fully process the pain of the past can hinder your ability to form genuine connections based on mutual respect and trust. When you are truly ready to open your heart to love again, it will be from a place of strength, authenticity, and wholeness, ensuring that you build your relationship on a solid foundation. Resist the temptation to seek love out of loneliness, knowing that when the time is right, love will find its way to you.

Day 351

What defines you is how you rise after falling.

Your true essence is not decided by the challenges you face, but by how you respond to them. Divorce is a profound test of resilience and strength, demanding that you summon the courage to rise again after falling. By refusing to be defined by your failures and setbacks, you reclaim your power and agency over your life, forging a path forward with determination and grace.

Day 352

If you are not proud of your life to this point,
be bold enough to start over, this time much better.

Feel inspired to strive for a life that you are proud of, one filled with purpose, fulfillment, and authenticity. If, upon reflection, you find you are not living up to your fullest potential, these words offer a reminder that it is never too late to make a change. They speak to the strength and resilience within each of us, urging us to find the courage to let go of what no longer serves us and start anew. They remind us that true strength lies not in avoiding failure or hardship, but in our ability to rise again, renewed and empowered, ready to chart a course toward a life that reflects our truest selves.

Day 353

Accept your past with no regrets, manage your present with confidence, and face your future with no fear.

Divorce often brings with it a whirlwind of emotions, regrets, and uncertainties about the future. Yet, amidst the chaos, there lies an opportunity for profound self-discovery and growth. These words remind us to embrace our past with acceptance and compassion, recognizing that every experience, no matter how challenging, has contributed to shaping who we are today. As we navigate the present moment, these words encourage us to approach each day with confidence and resilience, trusting in our own abilities to overcome obstacles and forge a path forward.

Day 354

At the end of the day, only time will heal your wounds.

Despite the desire for instant relief, true healing requires patience, resilience, and self-compassion. Like the mending of physical wounds, emotional healing takes time to repair the broken pieces of the heart and soul. Each passing day brings a measure of healing, as the sharp edges of pain gradually soften, and the sting of loss fades. It's about allowing yourself the space to grieve, to process, and to rebuild your life on your own terms.

Day 355

Once you're divorced, stop trying to take care of your former mate. They are not your responsibility anymore.

While it's natural to want to maintain some level of concern for their welfare, constantly trying to take care of your former spouse can hinder your ability to move forward. By focusing on your self-care and personal growth, you create space for both you and your ex-spouse to embrace new opportunities and experiences separate from the past relationship. Redirecting your energy toward building a fulfilling life for yourself allows you to let go of the role of caretaker and instead, embrace a sense of freedom and autonomy.

Day 356

Starting over is about giving yourself a chance at a future filled with real happiness.

Starting over requires courage, resilience, and a willingness to step into the unknown with an open heart and mind. It's about releasing yourself from the confines of regret and embracing the endless possibilities that lie ahead. Whether it's pursuing a new career path, cultivating meaningful relationships, or rediscovering passions long forgotten, starting over allows you to redefine what happiness means to you and to pursue it with unwavering determination.

Day 357

Do something today that your future self will appreciate.

Take a moment to imagine yourself six months or a year from now. Do you want to be in the same place, doing the same things? Is that something your future self will be proud you've started or accomplished? Now's the time to take the first step toward making that a reality. By prioritizing actions that align with your values and aspirations, you can lay the groundwork for a brighter and more fulfilling future.

Day 358

Review and realize what went wrong so you can avoid those things next time.

As part of your healing process, take the time to understand what led to the breakdown of the marriage. By identifying the factors that contributed to the divorce, you can take proactive steps to avoid repeating the same mistakes in future relationships. This self-awareness allows for greater emotional intelligence and maturity, fostering healthier connections and more fulfilling partnerships down the road. While the process of introspection may be challenging and even painful, it can lead to a deeper understanding of oneself and one's needs in a relationship.

Day 359

Regrets are a waste of time.

Dwelling on regrets is a self-imposed roadblock to personal growth and healing. Time spent fixating on past mistakes or missed opportunities detracts from the present moment and can stop you from positively moving forward. By accepting what has happened and embracing the lessons learned from the past, you can channel your energy into making positive changes. Letting go of regrets will free you from the burdens of the past and allow you to live more fully in the present, making the most of the opportunities that lie ahead.

Day 360

Build memories that have nothing to do with your past.

By intentionally creating new memories and forging fresh paths, you will rewrite the narrative of your life. Whether it's exploring new hobbies, embarking on solo adventures, or nurturing relationships with newfound friends, each memory becomes a stepping stone toward healing and growth. By focusing on the present moment and actively seeking opportunities for joy and fulfillment, you are laying the foundation for a future that is defined not by your past, but by the endless possibilities that lie ahead.

Day 361

*Sometimes, good things fall apart so
better things can fall together.*

While the end of a marriage may feel like the unraveling of something cherished, it can also mark the beginning of a new chapter filled with growth and opportunities. By letting go of what no longer serves you, you create space for new and better things to enter your life. This could mean finding a deeper sense of self-awareness and self-love, discovering new passions or pursuits, or building healthier relationships based on mutual respect and understanding.

Day 362

Old ways won't open new doors.

Amid divorce, it's tempting to rely on familiar routines and coping mechanisms, even if they no longer serve us well. However, realizing that old ways won't open new doors underscores the importance of embracing change and seeking fresh perspectives. Instead of clinging to outdated beliefs or behaviors that may have contributed to the breakdown of the marriage, it's essential to be open to new possibilities and approaches. This might involve seeking therapy or counseling to address underlying issues, exploring new interests or hobbies to rediscover oneself, or adopting healthier communication and coping strategies.

Day 363

Own every aspect of your life completely.
After all, it is yours and yours alone.

Rather than assigning blame or dwelling on past mistakes, accepting complete accountability empowers you to take control of your present circumstances and shapes your future. This mindset shift allows for introspection and self-reflection, fostering a deeper understanding of your actions, choices, and consequences. By acknowledging personal responsibility, you can find areas for improvement and implement positive changes. This approach promotes resilience, self-reliance, and a sense of ownership over your destiny. In divorce, taking 100% responsibility means recognizing one's role in the relationship dynamics and the outcome of the marriage, while also embracing the opportunity for personal growth and transformation.

Day 364

Life is not always about trying to fix something that is broken. Sometimes, it's about starting over and creating something better.

Instead of solely focusing on trying to repair or salvage a relationship that may no longer serve both parties, it's essential to recognize the potential for growth and positive change that comes with starting over. Embracing this mindset allows individuals to let go of past grievances and envision a future filled with new possibilities, personal growth, and greater fulfillment. By viewing divorce as a stepping stone to a brighter future, individuals can approach the process with optimism and resilience, harnessing the lessons learned from their previous experiences to build stronger, healthier relationships and pursue paths that align more closely with their values and aspirations.

Day 365

*Wisdom is the reward of experience and
should be shared.*

Dozens of real people like you and I shared the wisdom within this book using our trials and triumphs of life's journey. Each experience, whether joyful or challenging, contributes to the tapestry of wisdom that enriches our lives. By sharing our wisdom, we extend a hand to those who may be navigating a similar path, offering them guidance, comfort, and encouragement. In this sharing, we forge connections, weaving a web of collective understanding and empathy. Through the act of sharing, we not only honor the lessons learned, but also pay homage to the individuals whose experiences have shaped us. Embrace the responsibility to share our wisdom generously, recognizing that, in doing so, we not only enrich the lives of others, but also reaffirm the profound interconnectedness of the human experience.

What's Next?

Congratulations on completing this book filled with wisdom from real people! As you've journeyed through the pages, you've discovered the profound truth encapsulated in the quote:

Wisdom is the reward of experience and should be shared.

Your role as the bearer of these stories doesn't end here. Your journey is just beginning. Embrace the opportunity to continue sharing wisdom, and to uplift and inspire others on their own paths. Let this be a reminder that we should not hoard wisdom but generously share it with those in need.

So, my friend, as you close this book, carry its lessons forward. And remember, your experiences and life lessons are your wisdom. They are invaluable treasures waiting to be shared with the world. Let's continue to learn from one another, grow, and spread positive energy and wisdom wherever we go.

About the Author

Jen Fort is a writer, coach, and natural born encourager who believes wisdom shared can turn even the hardest seasons into steppingstones for the path forward. She gathers lessons from real people navigating life's toughest transitions and passes them along with honesty, humor, and heart. *From Divorce Mess to Happiness* was born from her desire to help others find hope, healing, and strength after heartbreak. Through her writing, Jen reminds readers that while divorce may change the story, it doesn't end it—life can be rebuilt with courage, joy, and new beginnings.

Visit www.iamjenfort.com to:

- Share your favorite nuggets of wisdom and perhaps have your wisdom included in future books

- Learn about upcoming book releases

- Find out how you can further benefit from Jen's life mission to encourage and share life's lessons!

www.ingramcontent.com/pod-product-compliance
Lightning Source LLC
Chambersburg PA
CBHW060502130626
46553CB00002B/386